THE TRUTH S

MW01598874

Evangelism
As God Intended

Roger Henri Trepanier

© 2015

This book is dedicated to all evangelists on earth whom God has raised for the gospel of His grace, and also to all believers who have a desire to see others come to know God in a personal way!

"I thank my God in all my remembrance of you, always offering prayer with joy in my every prayer for you all, in view of your participation in the gospel from the first day until now."

Philippians 1:3-5

**Other titles available from Roger Henri Trepanier in
The Truth Seeker's Library™ series:**

God Did Not Create Human Beings To Die... But To Live On...
Eternally!

Finding Comfort And Encouragement In The Promises Of God
In The Last Days

How We Know For Sure That We Are Living In The Last Days!

Have You Ever Wondered What Happens After Death?

An Introduction To The New World That Is Coming On The
Earth

Deeper Truths Of The Christian Life

**Other titles available from Roger Henri Trepanier in
The Practical Helps Library™ series:**

Learning to Overcome The Perplexities Of This Present Life

So, I Hear You Want To Work With Seniors?

INTRODUCTION

A good place to start is to look at defining some terms used in the title of this book. For instance, the word "evangelism" is not a Biblical word, since it does not occur anywhere in God's word, the Bible. The closest word which does appear in God's word is the word "evangelist," which literally refers to God's 'messenger of good,' a 'bringer of good tidings,' that is, a preacher of the gospel. The word "gospel" means 'good news,' so that an evangelist is someone who brings God's good news to mankind. That is why if one looks up the word "evangel" in an English dictionary, such as the Oxford Concise Dictionary, it will say that this word simply refers to 'the gospel' and that the word "evangelism" simply refers to 'the preaching of the gospel.'

What the foregoing has meant is that in the minds of many people, believers in particular, they have come to associate the preaching of the gospel as being the task of the evangelist. To a large degree, that is true. However, what also needs to be grasped is that all believers are called of God to share their faith with unbelievers, as God leads and provides opportunities. The only difference is that the evangelist has a public ministry from God, while those believers who are not evangelists do not. But more on this later in the book. This has only been brought up here in the Introduction in order to make the point that ALL believers have a responsibility before God to share their faith with others, not just one who is an evangelist.

As we will see later in the book, the gospel of God is concerning His own precious Son, our Lord Jesus Christ. From the beginning of creation, which is when time began, God set out to make Himself known to mankind, doing so through His Son. In other words, God cannot be known apart from knowing His Son in a personal way. This very important truth is not something any human being dreamed up, but rather God Himself has disclosed this to us, doing so in quite an enigmatic statement, noting what God's Son was led to say at Matthew 11:27, "All things have been handed over to Me by My Father; and no one knows the Son except the Father; nor does anyone know the Father except the Son, and anyone to whom the Son wills to reveal Him." An enigma simply means 'something which is puzzling,' and what is enigmatic here in God's statement is that God says that no one knows The Son except The Father, while at the same time, no one knows The Father except The Son! If that was all the information we had to go by then it would be easy for one to read this and say, 'then who can know God?' And so that is why God's Son was led to add at the end here, "and anyone to whom The Son wills to reveal Him." In other words, the only human beings who can know God The Father are those to whom The Son of God reveals Him to.

This then brings up the question: To whom does The Son of God reveal His Father to? And the answer to that question was given by The Son of God in an interchange which he had with one of His disciples one day, when on earth at His first coming from Heaven to earth, noting what we read at John 14:7-9, "[7] If you had known Me, you would have known My Father also; from now on you know Him, and have seen Him." [8] Philip said to Him, "Lord, show us the Father, and it is enough for us." [9] Jesus said to him, "Have I been so long with you, and yet you have not come to know Me, Philip? He who has seen Me has seen the Father; how can you say, 'Show us the Father'?" What God's precious Son, Jesus Christ, makes known to us at verse 7 here is that in one knowing Him, one not only also knew The Father, but one had now seen The Father also. As we see at verse 8, the disciple did not quite grasp this statement, so asks at verse 8 that The Son, who was now before them in human flesh, to show them The Father, which prompts The Son to answer at verse 9 by saying plainly, "He who has seen Me has seen The Father." Taking what The Son was led to say at verse 7 with verse 9 then, we learn that The Father can only be seen and known in seeing and knowing God's Son.

Now the only reason this fairly extended discussion was brought in here was to point out why it is so important for God to make His good news, the gospel, which is concerning His precious Son, made known to mankind, because it is only in knowing The Son in a personal relationship that one can know God The Father, from Whom are all things, especially the forgiveness of sins and eternal life, which is the whole point of what God wants to accomplish in time. In other words, God wants men and women to know Him so that one might have the forgiveness of sins and eternal life with Him now on earth, and then be with Him forever after this life!

And then what would also be helpful for one to know at the outset is that this book has been divided into five sections. The first section deals with the gospel, where we examine what it is, what is its primary focus, why is the gospel so important to God, ways of sharing the gospel, including Biblical examples where we see the gospel being shared. The second section deals with the subject of salvation, in terms of what it is, why is it so important to be saved, what is one being saved from, who is God's primary focus in salvation, also looking here at God's election and sovereignty, and the fact that salvation is to be seen as being wholly a work of God alone! The third section deals with evangelism, in terms of seeing what God intended to happen in evangelism, also seeing that God put forth His own Son as our Pattern for evangelism, while also looking closely at the preparation and the effectiveness of the vessels God delights to use in evangelism.

In the fourth section, we look closely at the role of the evangelist in relation to evangelism, in relation to the apostle, in relation to elders, and in relation to the teaching function in a local church. We also look at key truths which we need to remember regarding evangelists, before turning to look at men who were called "evangelists" in God's word, and also at some men who had some other form of ministry. In the fifth and last section, we look at common misconceptions regarding evangelism, such as what is the relation between repentance and faith, whether it only the evangelist who is called of God to do evangelism, and the fact that the word missionary is a misnomer. The book then closes with an Addendum, where we present a chapter on coming to know God in a personal way, for those reading the book who may not have such a relationship with our Creator, but who would like to.

What should also be mentioned before closing the Introduction is that after completing 21 years of formal education and then spending almost 28 years working in Project Engineering in the corporate offices of a large utility, God called His servant as an evangelist in early 1999, then sent him out over 2500 miles, away from family and friends, to the place of service God assigned, and where His servant has been and is still serving Him as evangelist, counselor, author, and publisher. This book, "Evangelism As God Intended" is the author's ninth published work. The author is a widower with three adopted children.

A website has been established for the purpose of interacting with readers, which can be found at:

http://www.pilgrimpathwaypublications.com

God also led His servant to establish another website specifically for gospel ministry, since the author is an evangelist. That website can be found at:

http://www.servantofmosthigh.com

And now my prayer is that God will richly bless you as you read this book, and that He will greatly minister to your every need in your life, as only God can!

CONTENTS

SECTION FOUR   THE ROLE OF THE EVANGELIST

**SECTION FIVE   CLEARING UP SOME
                        MISCONCEPTIONS RELATING TO
                        EVANGELISM**

ADDENDUM

TO PERSONALLY KNOW GOD IS THE BE ALL
AND END ALL FOR ALL HUMAN LIFE ON EARTH!

SECTION ONE

THE GOSPEL:
WHAT IT IS; WHAT IS ITS PRIMARY FOCUS; AND
WHY IT IS SO IMPORTANT TO GOD

WHAT IS THE GOSPEL?

We have seen from the Introduction already that the word "gospel" means 'good news.' And to be specific, we are not just talking about any type of good news which is regarded as such among humankind, but rather here we have in view God's own good news to mankind, which surpasses by far all good news we could possibly receive during this lifetime. For God's good news relates to and affects one's eternal destiny after this life. So this subject is not something to take lightly, but rather all humankind is to take this very seriously, especially if one reading this does not as yet know God in a personal relationship.

Therefore, relating to what the gospel is, the best approach here is to listen to what God says the gospel is, noting what He tells us at Romans 1:1-4, "[1] Paul, a bond-servant of Christ Jesus, called as an apostle, set apart for the gospel of God, [2] which He promised beforehand through His prophets in the holy Scriptures, [3] concerning His Son, who was born of a descendant of David according to the flesh, [4] who was declared the Son of God with power by the resurrection from the dead, according to the Spirit of holiness, Jesus Christ our Lord..." What God tells us starting at verse 1 here is that Paul was set apart by God as an apostle for the purpose of sharing "the gospel of God" to other human beings. Since we know already that the word "gospel" speaks of 'good news,' then this means that the gospel is simply God's good news to mankind. Then going on to verse 3 and 4, we further learn that God's good news to mankind concerns His Son, Who is "Jesus Christ our Lord." Therefore, the simplest statement that we can make about the gospel is that it is God's good news to mankind concerning His precious Son, Jesus Christ.

Key truth to remember:

The gospel is God's good news to mankind concerning His Son, Jesus Christ.

WHAT IS THE PRIMARY FOCUS OF THE GOSPEL?

In now having an understanding of what the gospel is, we can go on to learn what the primary focus of the gospel is, that is, what is the core message which God delights to use to bring a person to faith in Himself. And here it would be helpful to note what God tells us at 1 Corinthians 15:1-4, where we read, "[1] Now I make known to you, brethren, the gospel which I preached to you, which also you received, in which also you stand, [2] by which also you are saved, if you hold fast the word which I preached to you, unless you believed in vain. [3] For I delivered to you as of first importance what I also received, that Christ died for our sins according to the Scriptures, [4] and that He was buried, and that He was raised on the third day according to the Scriptures..." God specifically says here at verse 1 that He is making known to us the gospel, that is, what its core message is, which God refers to at verse 4 as being "of first importance."

And please also note again the truth being stated at verse 2, that it is the message of the gospel which God uses to save a person, with that taking place the very moment a person believes, and as we have seen already, this being the result of a work of God's grace and power alone. Then at verses 3 and 4, we have the core message of the gospel, which God wants an unbeliever to hear and to believe in order to be saved, that is, to receive God's forgiveness of all of one's sins and also His eternal life, which is His righteousness. And that core message is that Christ died for our sins, that He was buried, and that He was raised on the third day.

Key truth to remember:

The central message of the gospel, which an unbeliever will believe by God's grace and power at the moment of one coming to know God in salvation is that Christ died for our sins, that He was buried, and that He was raised from the dead the third day.

WHY IS THE GOSPEL SO IMPORTANT TO GOD?

Then as to why the gospel is so important to God, we can further note what God says to us at Romans 1:16,17, where we read, "[16] For I am not ashamed of the gospel, for it is the power of God for salvation to everyone who believes, to the Jew first and also to the Greek. [17] For in it the righteousness of God is revealed from faith to faith; as it is written, "But the righteous man shall live by faith." What God makes known in these verses is that the gospel is extremely important because it is God's only means of bringing a person who is in unbelief to faith in God, which is when God forgives all of one's sins and bestows His righteous life, which is His righteousness, for a person who now believes to live by. In other words, one cannot be saved from the penalty of death due one's sins apart from believing the gospel of God, which as we have seen is concerning His precious Son, Jesus Christ.

God says the same thing again to us this time in Scriptural language at Romans 3:21-24, where we read, "[21] But now apart from the Law the righteousness of God has been manifested, being witnessed by the Law and the Prophets, [22] even the righteousness of God through faith in Jesus Christ for all those who believe; for there is no distinction; [23] for all have sinned and fall short of the glory of God, [24] being justified as a gift by His grace through the redemption which is in Christ Jesus..." Please especially note verse 22, where we see clearly that God's righteous life comes the moment one believes in God's Son, our Lord Jesus Christ. This is the moment that a person is said to be saved from the penalty of death due to one's sins, in terms of having all of one's sins removed and being bestowed God's righteous life, that is, His righteousness, to now live by as a child of God. It is important to also note from verse 24 that this work being done in the person's life at the moment of salvation is a work which God does. In other words, salvation is the gift of God, which is when He brings a person, who hears the gospel of God, to believe it. God is pleased to use us as vessels to share the gospel, which He then uses to save precious souls for His honor, glory, and praise!

Please further note how God speaks of the importance of the gospel at Ephesians 1:13,14, "[13] In Him, you also, after listening to the message of truth, the gospel of your salvation — having also believed, you were sealed in Him with the Holy Spirit of promise, [14] who is given as a pledge of our inheritance, with a view to the redemption of God's own possession, to the praise of His glory." And so we see here that God calls the message of truth which each of us believed in coming to know God as "the gospel of your salvation," that is, the good news concerning His precious Son, Jesus Christ, which God used to bring us to faith in Himself, and render us a child of His forever.

Then please note one final truth here at verses 13 and 14 regarding The third Person of The Trinity, that being The Holy Spirit, Whom God gives in one's human spirit at the moment one believes the gospel as a work of God's grace and power. The Holy Spirit is God's guarantee of one being born as a child of God in His family now, and then to be with God in Heaven one day. It is just like a man and a woman exchanging rings at the wedding ceremony, where in effect the bride and groom are saying to each other, 'you are mine.' We too become God's children forever at salvation, with God giving His Holy Spirit as His way of sealing the transaction forever!

Key truth to remember:

The gospel is very important to God because it is by means of one believing the gospel that God brings a human being in unbelief into a personal relationship with Himself in salvation.

WAYS OF SHARING THE GOSPEL

Since the gospel is the message of God concerning His precious Son, Jesus Christ, centered on his death, burial, and resurrection from the dead, then it is clear that any way which conveys this to an unbeliever is a sharing of the gospel. Examples are here presented just to give the reader some ideas on how to go about doing this.

1) The gospel accounts for sharing the gospel

If one has read my book 'So, I Hear You Want To Work With Seniors?,' and especially the third section on ministering to seniors, one has likely noticed that I have personally read through the gospel accounts in the support groups which I have had among seniors in the last fifteen years. We need to be aware here that all four gospel accounts are concerning the life of God's Son while on earth at His first coming from Heaven to earth, and all four contain the details of His death, burial, and resurrection from the dead, which is the core message of the gospel. Many of the seniors who have come to faith in God in these support groups have been by this method. We need to remember here what God says about His word, the Bible, at Romans 10:17, where we read, "So faith comes from hearing, and hearing by the word of Christ." That is, faith comes from God to a person when one hears the good news of God concerning His precious Son, Jesus Christ!

What has just been said in regard to a senior support group is also applicable to any type of Bible study group, whether that be a couple's group, a women's group, or a men's group, in one's home, or elsewhere, for the important part is the reading of the gospel accounts containing the gospel, which God delights to use to bring precious souls to faith in Himself. Of course, it needs to be mentioned that at any time one is reading any portion of the gospel accounts to others, God may lead one to share the core of the gospel. One only needs to be sensitive to the leading of The precious Holy Spirit

What also needs to be remembered about the gospel accounts is that the gospel of John in particular has specifically been given by God to see precious souls come to know Him, since that gospel account focuses on the Deity of The Son of God. And here we can note what God Himself says at John 20:31 in regards to what His purpose was in giving this particular gospel account to mankind, "but these have been written so that you may believe that Jesus is the Christ, the Son of God; and that believing you may have life in His name." Therefore, be assured that whether it is one on one with an unbeliever, or whether one is with a whole group, one can read the gospel accounts to these persons, which God can then use to bring them to faith in Himself.

2) The use of a verse such as John 3:16 as a take-off verse for sharing the gospel

Another very good method for sharing the gospel, but which requires one to know the Bible fairly well, and some key verses related to the gospel in particular, is to use a verse such as John 3:16 as a take-off verse to give a presentation and explanation of the gospel. To give an example here, one can quote the verse, which is "For God so loved the world, that He gave His only begotten Son, that whoever believes in Him shall not perish, but have eternal life," and then one can say why God had to give His own precious Son, which then leads to talk about Adam and Eve and the fall of man into sin, with mankind incurring a sinful nature and the penalty of death, since the penalty for sin is death. Then one can quote Romans 5:12 at this point to amplify this truth, where we read, "Therefore, just as through one man (Adam) sin entered into the world, and death through sin, and so death spread to all men, because all sinned..." At this point one can return to why God had to send His own Son, as born of a virgin, in order to not incur that sinful nature of Adam, passed on from the male, which is why God prepared a body in the womb of the virgin, so that His eternal Son, Who was ever sinless, could remain sinless in taking on a body like ours in the innocence of Adam, so that He could die in our place as our Substitute, to pay the penalty of death due our sins.

Then we can return to John 3:16 and where we read, "whoever believes in Him," can be used to say what it is that God wants a person to believe in order not to perish and to have eternal life with God, quoting at this point the core of the gospel message found at 1 Corinthians 15:3,4, "[3] ...that Christ died for our sins according to the Scriptures, [4] and that He was buried, and that He was raised on the third day according to the Scriptures..."

Then in regards to the last part of John 3:16, one can say that one has only two roads in life leading to opposite destinies, where to believe in God's precious Son, Jesus Christ, is to be forgiven all of one's sins and to receive God's eternal life, so as to be with Him forever in Heaven one day; or else the other road leads one to perish, in terms of being separated from God forever in a real place of conscious torment called hell. Here one can quote a verse such as Romans 6:23, "For the wages of sin is death, but the free gift of God is eternal life in Christ Jesus our Lord," and also 1 Peter 3:18 in part, "For Christ also died for sins once for all, the just for the unjust, so that He might bring us to God..."

Then we can close our presentation by quoting Romans 10:13, "for "Whoever will call on the name of the Lord will be saved." " And at this point one can ask the person if they would like to call on God to receive the forgiveness of all of one's sins and to have eternal life with God. If God is leading them to be saved at this point, then they will say 'yes,' at which point one can just tell the person to bow one's head and pray to God audibly or silently. Even if a person does not come to know God at this point, one has at least heard the gospel, which God can use at a later date, even when the person is alone, as God can bring the truth previously heard back to one's memory.

Of course, there can be many variations to the above, with different verses being used as a take-off verse, such as 1 Peter 3:18 instead of John 3:16. Whatever take-off verse God leads one to use, the one thing which is nice about this method is that it can be used when there is not a lot of time available to share the gospel. All of the foregoing here can be shared in ten minutes or less, not as a memorized formula, but in giving The precious Holy Spirit room to work in terms of varying the verses to be used. One should always be Spirit-filled and Spirit-led in sharing the gospel, as this is what God intends.

Recently, I had a God-given opportunity over a four hour period to share God with a couple in their rental unit, which included sharing and explaining the gospel. When I left, the wife said that this was the best evening she had ever spent in her life. The husband said that this was the first time that he actually felt comfortable talking about God, for they were both in their mid-fifties, and he said that he had quite a number of people try to share God with him, but it always turned him off. I told him that the difference was that this was a God-appointed situation where I was allowing God to lead and speak through me, not forcing the conversation. The husband was even surprised at one point when I asked him if I he wanted me to stop. This is only mentioned here to point out that when the gospel is being shared as God intends, as a God-appointed situation, by one who is Spirit-filled and being led of God, then the hearers will never be turned off. It is only when we attempt to do God's work in our own strength apart from Him that we turn people off. The truth shared God's way always touches the heart of the hearers, whether they come to believe at that point or not!

3) Other tools for sharing the gospel

There are also other tools for sharing the gospel with unbelievers, which one can use, such as little booklets like "Steps To Peace With God," or many such booklets. There are also evangelistic messages on DVD, which one can have on one's laptop or tablet and then have a person or a group listen to. There are also evangelistic books, which one can lend or give to a person to read on one's own, such as the author's first book, which is titled, "God Did Not Create Human Beings To Die... But To Live On Eternally," this being an evangelistic book. There are also many personal testimonies which are evangelistic, which God can use to bring a person to faith in Himself. This chapter closes with my personal testimony as an example. There are also evangelistic websites where the gospel is being shared that one can direct unbelievers to. One example of this is my own evangelistic website, which God led His servant to establish at:

http://www.servantofmosthigh.com

One other important comment here, which is that as an evangelist, I am always being guided by The Holy Spirit as to where a person is spiritually and then in what to say to that person. In other words, when an evangelist shares the gospel with someone, the core of the gospel is always there, to be sure, but the surrounding material is never the same, for each person is at a different place in what they know about God already. What I mean to say is that as an evangelist, the gospel is never shared as if it were a formula, for The Holy Spirit leads and guides as to what to say based on where a person is spiritually, which only God knows. The Addendum is one example of this, which is based on an actual occurrence of where all this material was said to a person God was in the process of bringing to faith in Himself, as led by The Holy Spirit in me, all for God's honor, glory, and praise!

4) The value of a personal testimony

As mentioned above, we will now close this chapter with my own personal testimony, as an example of an evangelistic tool which God can use as part of His work in bringing a human being to faith in Himself. Over the last thirty-five years, God has led His servant to give His testimony many times, either orally or in writing, sometimes the longer version and sometimes a shortened version of it. Just to take one Biblical example here, we can note that the apostle Paul's testimony is related to us no less than three times by God in the book of Acts alone (Acts 9:1-22; 22:3-21; 26:9-23), with portions of his testimony being given in many portions of the letters of the New Testament.

I was born in what some would call 'a religious' home, meaning that my parents knew about God, but did not personally know Him, nor did they realize that God intended for human beings to have a personal relationship with Him, which was the reason He created us. My parents were poor probably largely due to the fact that my father never went to school in his life, never even knowing how to read or write until the time of his death. My mother went to grade six and did learn to read and write, so she looked after finances and all mail came to her. They were also probably poor in having had seven children to raise and then trying to subsist on only one salary. So we grew up with hand-me-downs and few of the material things of this life, including a lot of toys. What my parents lacked in wealth of this world, they made up for it in love. They both loved each and every one of us, and this, apart from the love of God in the gospel, was probably the best gift they could shower upon us. It sure provides for a good start to this life.

However, what became evident early on in my life was that I was a sinner and loved my sin. Even though my mother would often point to a picture of Jesus hanging in the kitchen while saying to all of us as we would eat our breakfast, "Be good now, for Jesus is watching," it was as if it fell on deaf ears, for the reality is that the more I tried to be good, the more I sinned! What I did not understand back then, of course, is that when the human race's first parents, Adam and Eve, sinned in the garden of Eden, they incurred a sinful nature, which has been passed on through the male to every human being born from then on. What this means is that every human being is a sinner from the age of accountability onwards, that being the age at which as a child knows the good and the evil, and chooses the evil, thereby becoming personally accountable to God for one's sin. The fact that the whole of the human race have become sinners by nature and by practice since the time of Adam and Eve is made clear by God in what He says at Romans 5:12, "Therefore, just as through one man (Adam) sin entered into the world, and death through sin, and so death spread to all men, because all sinned..." (from the age of accountability onwards).

And so during my early years I was caught between wanting to please my mother by being good, but constantly falling short by continually sinning. That sinning included what I cannot mention here, as I am too ashamed of what I did, plus it would not serve any purpose, since this is a testimony, and not a tabloid. Two things I will mention, though, one is that I started drinking and smoking when I was nine, and at the age of ten I had a parting of ways with God. What I mean by this is that when I was ten I was fed up with God, for I concluded that it was impossible for me to be good on my own, so why continue with God. So one day while walking home – and I still remember that day – I shook my little fist at God and swore at Him with every swear word that I had learned by then, which was substantial. I also said to God to leave me alone! And do you know what, He did for the next 17 years. Now when I sinned, I had no thought of God, in terms of whether it was right or wrong, nor of trying to be good. I just went from one sin to another as a normal part of my life. Looking back over that period of my life, there is only one word to describe it – difficulties! God would leave me alone alright, but my life would be difficult and fraught with problems.

What I am thankful for now is that God did not leave me in my misery, but was mindful of my ignorance of Him. For when I was 27, I was sitting in a pew in the church of the religious system I had been brought up in, and concluded that Sunday evening that God was not in that place! What this meant then is that when I left that church building that evening, I would be on a quest to find and know this God, Whom I only knew about, but did not personally know. And that search would lead me to explore other religious systems and philosophies of life, which only left me yearning. I read somewhere that every human being born into this world is born with a hole in one's heart, which only God can fill. And until He does, all we do is go on yearning, never finding peace until God fills that hole! Have you ever experienced that yourself?

Another thing which happened when I was 27 is that I went back to school. I had already graduated with a degree in Engineering by then and had been working in the Engineering department of a large utility for about five years. Since I had the same ambition as any other young man in my position in those days, which was to get rich and be President of the Company, then that meant in my own mind going back to school and getting more education. And it was while I was in one of those classes that I first laid eyes on the most beautiful woman I had ever seen. But whenever I approached her, I just froze. What I did not realize back then is that I was about to come into contact with the very first person I had ever met in my life who was a Christian, that is, one who had a personal relationship with this God I was by now trying to discover for myself. One night, during a coffee break in the night class, I actually got enough nerve to sit at the same table as this young woman, whom I found out later was 25. At least we exchanged names that night, although we already knew that from class.

It was not until the next semester in the spring that I got enough nerve to ask this young woman out. When I went to class for 7 pm that night, I had already had five beers, since I had been entertaining a co-worker from out of town after work. So I went to class that evening with a little less inhibition than normal. So when I left the school building that night and saw this young woman waiting for the bus outside, I asked her if I could drive her home. I was in high heaven when she said 'yes,' and all the way to her place, since we talked freely now, with one thing that I found out was that she was from out of the city, only renting a cottage by the lake. So when we arrived at the cottage, I was surprised, but pleased, when she invited me in for coffee. What I did not know is that her mother was there, which is why she felt safe in inviting me in. And she had not finished putting a cup of coffee in front of me before she started telling me that she was a Christian, and then went on to talk about Jesus Christ as if it was someone she knew very well. All I knew of Him at this time is that we had a picture of Him on the wall in my parent's home, which still hung there, and that somehow He was connected to The God Whom I had swore at 17 years earlier, but Whom I was now trying to know. Since I had a sense of humor, I pulled out my wallet at that point and showed her a picture of a former girlfriend and told her that this was my wife. Then I pulled out a picture of a few nieces and nephews and said these were my kids. I do not think I convinced her, for when I left later, she got up and walked me to my car. Since she had done that, then I knew that she had some interest in me, so I asked her if her mom was still going to be there that Saturday night. When she said no, then I asked her out for an evening meal in a restaurant. This date led to a two year relationship, in which I never did get to kiss her, and every time I picked her up, she would only allow me in the cottage if we could read the Bible together. Since I had never opened a Bible in my life, then that meant that I only walked her to the door. I did meet her father and one of her brothers. The other one was working out West.

In the spring of my 29th birthday, she graduated with a teaching degree and moved out West after accepting a teaching position where her brother was. For my part, I was still working by day and going to school in the evening, working on a second degree. I had just been made a Supervisor at work, which meant I now had a Company car, my own office, my own secretary and staff. It also meant that I had to travel. And so on October 10th in my 29th year on this earth, I found myself for the very first time in my life picking up a Bible in a hotel room. Normally they have a Gideon Bible, but this hotel had New Testaments from the Home Bible League. That was about 8:45 pm in the evening when I started reading and I read until 11 pm. Then I noticed inside that it said that one could take it home if one sent them two dollars and told them which room and which hotel it had been taken from. So I left the next morning with the only Bible I had ever cracked open in my life. I got home that Friday evening not knowing that God was drawing me to Himself. In other words, I thought that it was me who was searching for Him, while all the time it was God Who was drawing me to Himself. It was only later that I would read this truth at John 6:44, where Jesus told a crowd one day, "No one can come to Me unless the Father who sent Me draws him..." In fact, in the next few days I read not only this verse, but the whole of the New Testament. When I finished reading, I was caught between two opinions, which were that either this Jesus was The Son of God, as He claimed to be, or else He was just a religious impostor, which was what the religious leaders of His day made Him out to be.

And that is where I was when I received a care package from my girlfriend out West in early December. Inside the fairly large box were all kinds of goodies to eat, plus a letter, plus a little tract, called "Steps To Peace With God." I read the letter, ate the snacks, and threw the tract on my dresser top, without reading it. Then at Christmas time, I did what I normally did every other year, which was to go to my parent's house and join in all the parties that were going on with relatives, plus do a lot of drinking. But that Christmas was different, and everyone noticed. It was like there was a heavy wet blanket that had been spread over me. I was humorless and did not feel like partying. Sure did not seem like me at all. What I did not know was that I was now under a deep conviction of sin, which was also part of God's doing in drawing me to Himself, so that I would come to realize within myself that what God says at Romans 3:23 is indeed true, "for all have sinned and fall short of the glory of

God." By the time I drove home after the New Years, I knew without a doubt that this verse described me very well!

Where I was living at the time was in a very large apartment complex, where the superintendent and his family had become friends of mine. What I did not realize at the time was that the man and his family were Christians. So on Saturday, January 12th of my 29th year – I would not be turning 30 until February 13th – I found myself in the car with the superintendent, going to a businessman's breakfast. These were Christian businessmen in the city who were putting on these breakfasts for the purpose of reaching other men with the gospel of God. There are only two things I remember about that morning, one being two verses from the Bible which another Christian man shared with me that morning, from Proverbs 3:5,6, "[5] Trust in the Lord with all your heart and do not lean on your own understanding. [6] In all your ways acknowledge Him, and He will make your paths straight." The other was a testimony like this one, which a man shared, relating to how he came to know God.

So there I was on the next Monday evening, which was January 14th, alone in my apartment as I got home from work. I did not feel like eating, so I just sat in my big comfort chair pondering that critical question of who was Jesus? Was He really The Son of God come in human flesh, who lived a sinless life, then died on the cross the death that was due my sins, since the wages of sin is death? Or was He an impostor, as the religious leaders of His day made Him out to be? It was while I was pondering this that the thought came - no doubt from God, although at the time I did not know it – to go get that little booklet, "Steps To Peace With God," which my girlfriend had sent me, and which was still on top of my dresser. Now was God's timing to read this, for in that little booklet, the gospel was shared and illustrated, namely that Jesus had died to pay the penalty due my sins, that He was buried, and then was raised from the dead on the third day. When I came to the short prayer at the end, I prayed it, and as I prayed it, it was as if God was in the room with me, unseen but His Presence was felt down to the deepest part of my being, with His standing there in the room and extending a Hand for me to take. The next moment all my sins were lifted from me, and I felt a huge burden had been lifted from my shoulders. At the same time, such peace filled my heart that I just cried out over and over again, "Oh, dear God, do not leave, do not leave me!" I was so afraid that God was going to leave me that I kept saying this to myself over and over again. I remember coming home the next evening, still saying this to God. I figure that He was getting tired of hearing this from His new child now born into His family for all of a sudden I could not say it anymore, with God having now given me the assurance of my salvation, in terms of making me realize that He would never leave me, nor forsake me.

On January 14th, 2015, dear reader, it has been 35 years since that glorious event took place, and I can still remember it as if it took place yesterday. Who can ever forget such an event, when God grants one peace with Himself which passes understanding. Who can forget going from eternal death to eternal life, as God's Son promises at John 5:24, "Truly, truly, I say to you, he who hears My word, and believes Him who sent Me, has eternal life, and does not come into judgment, but has passed out of death into life." What God had also now done was to fill that hole in my heart with Himself. He had forgiven me of all my sins committed against Him since my childhood days, including all my little tirade and string of swear words which I had swore at Him in my ignorance at the age of ten, and had now written my name in Heaven in giving me eternal life with Him. What a merciful, forgiving, and loving God He is! To God be all praise, all honor, and glory, both now and forevermore! Amen.

BIBLICAL EXAMPLES OF THE SHARING OF THE GOSPEL

What would be helpful for learning to share the gospel is to look at the gospel messages which were preached to unbelievers by the apostles in the New Testament, specifically by Peter and Paul in Acts, which God caused to then be included as part of His word, which is not surprising since God was The One speaking through these men in the first place. One thing we will observe in looking at these gospel messages is noting that the core of the gospel is always included, namely that Christ died for our sins, that He was buried, and that He rose again from the dead, although at times His burial is simply understood. A brief commentary is included at the end of each gospel message showing that God's precious Son is in view as The One being preached, also giving the verses where His death and subsequent resurrection from the dead is being mentioned.

1) Peter's gospel message at Acts 2:22-41

"[22] Men of Israel, listen to these words: Jesus the Nazarene, a man attested to you by God with miracles and wonders and signs which God performed through Him in your midst, just as you yourselves know — [23] this Man, delivered over by the predetermined plan and foreknowledge of God, you nailed to a cross by the hands of godless men and put Him to death. [24] But God raised Him up again, putting an end to the agony of death, since it was impossible for Him to be held in its power. [25] For David says of Him, 'I saw the Lord always in my presence; for He is at my right hand, so that I will not be shaken. [26] Therefore my heart was glad and my tongue exulted; moreover my flesh also will live in hope; [27] because You will not abandon my soul to Hades, nor allow Your Holy One to undergo decay. [28] You have made known to me the ways of life; You will make me full of gladness with Your presence.' [29] Brethren, I may confidently say to you regarding the patriarch David that he both died and was buried, and his tomb is with us to this day. [30] And so, because he was a prophet and knew that God had sworn to him with an oath to seat one of his descendants on his throne, [31] he looked ahead and spoke of the resurrection of the Christ, that He was neither abandoned to Hades, nor did His flesh suffer decay. [32] This Jesus God raised up again, to which we are all witnesses. [33] Therefore having been exalted to the right hand of God, and having received from the Father the promise of the Holy Spirit, He has poured forth this which you both see and hear. [34] For it was not David who ascended into heaven, but he himself says: 'The Lord said to my Lord, "Sit at My right hand, [35] until I make Your enemies a footstool for Your feet." ' [36] Therefore let all the house of Israel know for certain that God has made Him both Lord and Christ — this Jesus whom you crucified." [37] Now when they heard this, they were pierced to the heart, and said to Peter and the rest of the apostles, "Brethren, what shall we do?" [38] Peter said to them, "Repent, and each of you be baptized in the name of Jesus Christ for the forgiveness of your sins; and you will receive the gift of the Holy Spirit. [39] For the promise is for you and your children and for all who are far off, as many as the Lord our God will call to Himself." [40] And with many other words he solemnly testified and kept on exhorting them, saying, "Be saved from this perverse generation!" [41] So then, those who had received his word were baptized; and that day there were added about three thousand souls."

What we need to observe here is that God's Son is mentioned by name at verses 22,31,32,36, and 38, as The One Who is being preached, with His death being mentioned at verses 23 and 36, with His resurrection from the dead being mentioned at verses 24,31, and 32.

2) Peter's gospel message at Acts 3:12-26

"[3] But when Peter saw this, he replied to the people, "Men of Israel, why are you amazed at this, or why do you gaze at us, as if by our own power or piety we had made him walk? [13] The God of Abraham, Isaac and Jacob, the God of our fathers, has glorified His servant Jesus, the one whom you delivered and disowned in the presence of Pilate, when he had decided to release Him. [14] But you disowned the Holy and Righteous One and asked for a murderer to be granted to you, [15] but put to death the Prince of life, the one whom God raised from the dead, a fact to which we are witnesses. [16] And on the basis of

34

faith in His name, it is the name of Jesus which has strengthened this man whom you see and know; and the faith which comes through Him has given him this perfect health in the presence of you all. [17] And now, brethren, I know that you acted in ignorance, just as your rulers did also. [18] But the things which God announced beforehand by the mouth of all the prophets, that His Christ would suffer, He has thus fulfilled. [19] Therefore repent and return, so that your sins may be wiped away, in order that times of refreshing may come from the presence of the Lord; [20] and that He may send Jesus, the Christ appointed for you, [21] whom heaven must receive until the period of restoration of all things about which God spoke by the mouth of His holy prophets from ancient time. [22] Moses said, 'The Lord God will raise up for you a prophet like me from your brethren; to Him you shall give heed to everything He says to you. [23] And it will be that every soul that does not heed that prophet shall be utterly destroyed from among the people.' [24] And likewise, all the prophets who have spoken, from Samuel and his successors onward, also announced these days. [25] It is you who are the sons of the prophets and of the covenant which God made with your fathers, saying to Abraham, 'And in your seed all the families of the earth shall be blessed.' [26] For you first, God raised up His Servant and sent Him to bless you by turning every one of you from your wicked ways."

Here we note that God's precious Son is in view by name at verses 13,16,18, and 20, with His death and resurrection from the dead being mentioned at verse 15.

3) Peter's gospel message at Acts 4:8-12

"[8] Then Peter, filled with the Holy Spirit, said to them, "Rulers and elders of the people, [9] if we are on trial today for a benefit done to a sick man, as to how this man has been made well, [10] let it be known to all of you and to all the people of Israel, that by the name of Jesus Christ the Nazarene, whom you crucified, whom God raised from the dead — by this name this man stands here before you in good health. [11] He is the stone which was rejected by you, the builders, but which became the chief corner stone. [12] And there is salvation in no one else; for there is no other name under heaven that has been given among men by which we must be saved."

In this gospel message, which although short, nevertheless has God's precious Son clearly mentioned by name at verse 10, while His death and resurrection from the dead is also mentioned at verse 10.

4) Peter's gospel message at Acts 5:29-32

"[29] But Peter and the apostles answered, "We must obey God rather than men. [30] The God of our fathers raised up Jesus, whom you had put to death by hanging Him on a cross. [31 He is the one whom God exalted to His right hand as a Prince and a Savior, to grant repentance to Israel, and forgiveness of sins. [32] And we are witnesses of these things; and so is the Holy Spirit, whom God has given to those who obey Him."

Again, a very short gospel message, but which nevertheless clearly identifies at verse 30 God's Son as The One being preached, with His death and resurrection from the dead being mentioned at verse 30 also.

5) Peter's gospel message at Acts 10:34-44

"[34] Opening his mouth, Peter said: "I most certainly understand now that God is not one to show partiality, [35] but in every nation the man who fears Him and does what is right is welcome to Him. [36] The word which He sent to the sons of Israel, preaching peace through Jesus Christ (He is Lord of all) — [37] you yourselves know the thing which took place throughout all Judea, starting from Galilee, after the baptism which John proclaimed. [38] You know of Jesus of Nazareth, how God anointed Him with the Holy Spirit and with power, and how He went about doing good and healing all who were oppressed by the devil, for God was with Him. [39] We are witnesses of all the things He did both in the land of the Jews and in Jerusalem. They also put Him to death by hanging Him on a cross. [40] God raised Him up on the third day and granted that He become visible, [41] not to all the people, but to witnesses who were chosen beforehand by God, that is, to us who ate and drank with Him after He arose from the dead. [42] And He ordered us to preach to the people, and solemnly to testify that this is the One who has been appointed by God as Judge of the living and the dead. [43] Of Him all the prophets bear witness that through His name everyone who believes in Him receives forgiveness of sins." [44] While Peter was still speaking these words, the Holy Spirit fell upon all those who were listening to the message."

Here also we see God's precious Son being mentioned by name at verses 36 and 38, with His death being mentioned at verse 39 and His resurrection from the dead at verses 40 and 41.

6) Paul's gospel message at Acts 13:16-41

"[16] Paul stood up, and motioning with his hand said, "Men of Israel, and you who fear God, listen: [17] The God of this people Israel chose our fathers and made the people great during their stay in the land of Egypt, and with an uplifted arm He led them out from it. [18] For a period of about forty years He put up with them in the wilderness. [19] When He had destroyed seven nations in the land of Canaan, He distributed their land as an inheritance — all of which took about four hundred and fifty years. [20] After these things He gave them judges until Samuel the prophet. [21] Then they asked for a king, and God gave them Saul the son of Kish, a man of the tribe of Benjamin, for forty years. [22] After He had removed him, He raised up David to be their king, concerning whom He also testified and said, 'I have found David the son of Jesse, a man after My heart, who will do all My will.' [23] From the descendants of this man, according to promise, God has brought to Israel a Savior, Jesus, [24] after John had proclaimed before His coming a baptism of repentance to all the people of Israel. [25] And while John was completing his course, he kept saying, 'What do you suppose that I am? I am not He. But behold, one is coming after me the sandals of whose feet I am not worthy to untie.' [26] Brethren, sons of Abraham's family, and those among you who fear God, to us the message of this salvation has been sent. [27] For those who live in Jerusalem, and their rulers, recognizing neither Him nor the utterances of the prophets which are read every Sabbath, fulfilled these by condemning Him. [28] And though they found no ground for putting Him to death, they asked Pilate that He be executed. [29] When they had carried out all that was written concerning Him, they took Him down from the cross and laid Him in a tomb. [30] But God raised Him from the dead; [31] and for many days He appeared to those who came up with Him from Galilee to Jerusalem, the very ones who are now His witnesses to the people. [32] And we preach to you the good news of the promise made to the fathers, [33] that God has fulfilled this promise to our children in that He raised up Jesus, as it is also written in the second Psalm, 'You are My Son; today i have begotten You.' [34] As for the fact that He raised Him up from the dead, no longer to return to decay, He has spoken in this way: 'I will give you the holy and sure blessings of David.' [35] Therefore He also says in another Psalm, 'You will not allow Your Holy One to undergo decay.' [36] For David, after he had served the purpose of God in his own generation, fell asleep, and was laid among his fathers and underwent decay; [37] but He whom God raised did not undergo decay. [38] Therefore let it be known to you, brethren, that through Him forgiveness of sins is proclaimed to you, [39] and through Him everyone who believes is freed from all things, from which you could not be freed through the Law of Moses. [40] Therefore take heed, so that the thing spoken of in the Prophets may not come upon you: [41] 'Behold, you scoffers, and marvel, and perish; for I am accomplishing a work in your days, a work which you will never believe, though someone should describe it to you.' "

In this gospel message by the apostle Paul, we have God's Son in view at verses 23 and 33 as The One being preached, with His death being mentioned at verses 28 and 29, while His resurrection from the dead is mentioned at verses 30,33,34, and 37. Here we also have His burial mentioned at verse 29, which we have seen so far has been generally only understood to have occurred.

7) Paul's gospel message at Acts 17:2-4

'[2] And according to Paul's custom, he went to them, and for three Sabbaths reasoned with them from the Scriptures, [3] explaining and giving evidence that the Christ had to suffer and rise again from the dead, and saying, "This Jesus whom I am proclaiming to you is the Christ." [4] And some of them were persuaded and joined Paul and Silas, along with a large number of the God-fearing Greeks and a number of the leading women."

Here we are to note that it was "Paul's custom" to preach the gospel as indicated here, making sure that God's Son was identified as The One being preached and was also The One Who died and rose again from the dead, as we see at verse 3.

8) Paul's gospel message at Acts 26:1-23

"[1] Agrippa said to Paul, "You are permitted to speak for yourself." Then Paul stretched out his hand and proceeded to make his defense: [2] "In regard to all the things of which I am accused by the Jews, I consider myself fortunate, King Agrippa, that I am about to make my defense before you today; [3] especially because you are an expert in all customs and questions among the Jews; therefore I beg you to listen to me patiently. [4] So then, all Jews know my manner of life from my youth up, which from the beginning was spent among my own nation and at Jerusalem; [5] since they have known about me for a long time, if they are willing to testify, that I lived as a Pharisee according to the strictest sect of our religion. [6] And now I am standing trial for the hope of the promise made by God to our fathers; [7] the promise to which our twelve tribes hope to attain, as they earnestly serve God night and day. And for this hope, O King, I am being accused by Jews. [8] Why is it considered incredible among you people if God does raise the dead? [9] So then, I thought to myself that I had to do many things hostile to the name of Jesus of Nazareth. [10] And this is just what I did in Jerusalem; not only did I lock up many of the saints in prisons, having received authority from the chief priests, but also when they were being put to death I cast my vote against them. [11] And as I punished them often in all the synagogues, I tried to force them to blaspheme; and being furiously enraged at them, I kept pursuing them even to foreign cities. [12] While so engaged as I was journeying to Damascus with the authority and commission of the chief priests, [13] at midday, O King, I saw on the way a light from heaven, brighter than the sun, shining all around me and those who were journeying with me. [14] And when we had all fallen to the ground, I heard a voice saying to me in the Hebrew dialect, 'Saul, Saul, why are you persecuting Me? It is hard for you to kick against the goads.' [15] And I said, 'Who are You, Lord?' And the Lord said, 'I am Jesus whom you are persecuting. [16] But get up and stand on your feet; for this purpose I have appeared to you, to appoint you a minister and a witness not only to the things which you have seen, but also to the things in which I will appear to you; [17] rescuing you from the Jewish people and from the Gentiles, to whom I am sending you, [18] to open their eyes so that they may turn from darkness to light and from the dominion of Satan to God, that they may receive forgiveness of sins and an inheritance among those who have been sanctified by faith in Me.' [19] So, King Agrippa, I did not prove disobedient to the heavenly vision, [20] but kept declaring both to those of Damascus first, and also at Jerusalem and then throughout all the region of Judea, and even to the Gentiles, that they should repent and turn to God, performing deeds appropriate to repentance. [21] For this reason some Jews seized me in the temple and tried to put me to death. [22] So, having obtained help from God, I stand to this day testifying both to small and great, stating nothing but what the Prophets and Moses said was going to take place; [23] that the Christ was to suffer, and that by reason of His resurrection from the dead He would be the first to proclaim light both to the Jewish people and to the Gentiles."

What is interesting about the apostle Paul's sharing of the gospel here is that it is contained as part of a word of testimony regarding when he first came into a personal relationship with God. And here we can note that God's precious Son is mentioned by name at verse 9, and that His death and resurrection from the dead is mentioned at verse 23.

What is revealing about the above gospel messages is that although all of them contain the core of the gospel, none of them is said in exactly the same way. And we are also to notice that some are long and some are short, but the important thing is that in each instance The One being preached is mentioned, with the core of the gospel being shared, and the speakers speaking as God was leading one to speak. May we all learn from the examples God gave us in His holy and precious word!

TRUTH IS JUST A STRING OF WORDS UNTIL
ILLUMINED TO THE HEART AND MIND BY THE
SPIRIT OF GOD!

SECTION TWO

SALVATION:
WHAT DOES IT MEAN; WHAT IS ONE BEING SAVED FROM; WHY IT IS SO IMPORTANT; AND WHO IS ITS PRIMARY FOCUS

WHAT DOES IT MEAN TO BE SAVED?

In looking at Ephesians 1:13 in the previous Section, we saw that God made reference to "the gospel of your salvation." Now that we have a basic understanding of what the gospel is, it is also important to know what this salvation is, which God also has in view. And one of the important things to remember about this word "salvation" in the Bible is that although there are different meanings, its principal meaning is that of deliverance. In the Old Testament, this deliverance by God is almost exclusively relating to deliverance from literal enemies, but in the New Testament, this deliverance by God is almost exclusively relating to deliverance which is part of a spiritual work which God does in salvation. What this means then is that the title of this chapter could also have been given as "what does it mean to be delivered." In this book and in this chapter then, we will look at salvation as being a spiritual deliverance by God, given by Him as a gift of His grace to one who believes God's good news regarding His Son, doing so under the following five headings:

1) A personal relationship with God

One important truth we need to know in regards to salvation, which is the result of believing the gospel as a work of God's grace and power alone, is that one who was formerly an unbeliever now enters into a personal relationship with God, which is eternal from the moment of believing the gospel of God's grace. It is very important that this be clear in our minds at the beginning here, namely that this personal relationship which we enter in with God at salvation is an eternal one, which can never be broken, as will be made clear as we continue. Before the moment of our salvation, although we may have known a lot about God, yet we did not know Him personally, as we do now.

2) The gift of The Holy Spirit

A second very important truth about salvation is that the moment one believes the gospel, which is always a result of God's grace and power, one receives from God the gift of His Holy Spirit (Acts 11:15-17), which as we have seen from

Ephesians 1:14 in the previous Section, is now the seal of God's personal guarantee to us that we can be sure of being with Him in Heaven one day. And so, the moment one believes God's central message regarding His Son, namely that He has died for our sins, was buried, and then was raised from the dead the third day, then God freely gives His Holy Spirit to indwell in one's human spirit forever. God's Son made this truth about The Holy Spirit clear when He told His disciples at John 14:16,17, "[16] I will ask the Father, and He will give you another Helper, that He may be with you forever; [17] that is the Spirit of truth, whom the world cannot receive, because it does not see Him or know Him, but you know Him because He abides with you and will be in you." Our conversing with God is through His Son by the enablement of The Holy Spirit from the moment of our salvation onward. And God's teaching of us is through His Son by The Holy Spirit in our human spirit.

3) A spiritual birth into God's family

What salvation also means is that one is now spiritually and eternally born into God's family. Since God is a spirit Being (John 4:24), and since Heaven is a spiritual place (John 18:36; 1 Corinthians 15:46-49), then we need a spiritual birth to become a child of God and to enter Heaven. This spiritual birth into God's family is what God refers to as being "born again" at John 3, where the term first occurs in Gods word, noting what God's Son said in this regard at John 3:1-8, "[1] Now there was a man of the Pharisees, named Nicodemus, a ruler of the Jews; [2] this man came to Jesus by night and said to Him, "Rabbi, we know that You have come from God as a teacher; for no one can do these signs that You do unless God is with him." [3] Jesus answered and said to him, "Truly, truly, I say to you, unless one is born again he cannot see the kingdom of God." [4] Nicodemus said to Him, "How can a man be born when he is old? He cannot enter a second time into his mother's womb and be born, can he?" [5] Jesus answered, "Truly, truly, I say to you, unless one is born of water and the Spirit he cannot enter into the kingdom of God. [6] That which is born of the flesh is flesh, and that which is born of the Spirit is spirit. [7] Do not be amazed that I said to you, 'You must be born again.' [8] The wind blows where it wishes and you hear the sound of it, but do not know where it comes from and where it is going; so is everyone who is born of the Spirit." We are to note very carefully that at verse 3 here, God's Son says that one cannot even see the Kingdom of God unless one is born again. Why? Because the Kingdom of God is a spiritual realm and so one needs a spiritual birth, which is what "born again" refers to. Then at verse 5, God's Son provides more information in regards to what being born again refers to when He states that "unless one is born of water and the Spirit he cannot enter into the kingdom of God." In other words, being born again is the result of the action of the word of God, the gospel, here referred to as the "water," being applied by The Holy Spirit to the heart and mind of a person, resulting in that person being born again, where one is cleansed of all sins and filled with the life of God to live by.

It would be helpful for us to look at two other verses of God's word at this point, first noting what God says to us at 1 Peter 1:23, where we read, "for you have been born again not of seed which is perishable but imperishable, that is, through the living and enduring word of God," and then also noting what God says to us at John 6:63, where we read, "It is the Spirit who gives life; the flesh profits nothing; the words that I have spoken to you are spirit and are life." And so we see that when a person is in the process of being brought into a personal relationship with God, The Holy Spirit takes the central message of the gospel, which the person would have heard, and applies it to the mind and heart of the person so that one now believes it, resulting in being born into God's family as The Holy Spirit comes to indwell into one's human spirit at the moment of believing the gospel. And this is exactly what we are told happens at John 3:8 above in the words, "so is everyone who is born of the Spirit." In other words, one is born again, this time into God's family, when one is born of The Spirit of God. Just as we needed a physical birth through our mother in order to enter this physical world, so too we need to have a spiritual birth by means of The Holy Spirit leading us to believe the gospel and then come to indwell our human spirit, so that now we can be born spiritually into God's family and be ready to enter God's Kingdom.

4) The forgiveness of sins

What also occurs at the moment of salvation, which is at the moment The precious Holy Spirit comes to indwell in one's human spirit, is that all of one's sins are forgiven! What this means is that all the sins that one has committed against God – and all sin is to be seen as being against God, Psalm 51:4 – since the age of accountability are now forgiven by God due to one having now believed the gospel and especially that when God's precious Son, Jesus Christ, died at the cross, he was there bearing the sins of the whole human race and therefore died the penalty due our sins, which was death. And the age of accountability here is to be seen as being when as a child, any of us and all of us as human beings, upon learning the right from the wrong, we personally chose the wrong, thereby having personally sinned against God and so becoming personally accountable to God for that sin committed against Him.

One passage of God's words, which would be helpful to look at here in order to see that God indeed does forgive one's sins at the moment of salvation would be Colossians 1:12-14, where we read, "[12] giving thanks to the Father, who has qualified us to share in the inheritance of the saints in Light. [13] For He rescued us from the domain of darkness, and transferred us to the kingdom of His beloved Son, [14] in whom we have redemption, the forgiveness of sins." At the moment of salvation, God The Father transfers us from the dominion of Satan, the devil (1 John 5:19), and transfers us to His own Kingdom, which during time is ruled by His Son, forgiving us of all our sins as He does so.

Two other verses which we can also mention here which bring out the truth of God forgiving one's sins at the moment of salvation is noting what we read at Acts 10:43, ""Of Him (that is, God's precious Son) all the prophets bear witness that through His name everyone who believes in Him receives forgiveness of sins." And here we see that the moment one believes in God's Son, namely the central message of the gospel concerning Him, being that He died for our sins, was buried, and rose again from the dead the third day, one receives the forgiveness of all of one's sins committed against God. Then the other verse which is very important to note here is Hebrews 9:22, where we read, "And according to the Law, one may almost say, all things are cleansed with blood, and without shedding of blood there is no forgiveness." The critical truth which God brings out here in the words, "without shedding of blood there is no forgiveness," is that the blood of His own Son, Jesus Christ, was shed unto death for us all, when He died at the cross, so that His death on the behalf of the whole human race is now the basis by which God forgives the sins of any who believes the gospel relating to His precious Son.

5) The reception of eternal life with God

We have already mentioned earlier in this chapter that one receives The precious Holy Spirit in one's human spirit at the moment of one's salvation. Now we are to see that in giving us His Holy Spirit to dwell in us, God The Father begins to impart His own righteous life for us to live by from the moment of our salvation onwards. In other words, from the moment of our salvation onward, God desires those who are now His children through a spiritual birth to now live only by His righteous life, which is His righteousness. Up to that moment of time, one has only lived by our own self life, living only for self. Now God wants one to live only for God, which one is now enabled to do by means of the imparted righteousness of God, coming through His Son to us by The Holy Spirit in one's spirit.

One key passage which would be helpful to look at here which focuses on the truth mentioned above is noting what God says at Romans 8:9-11, where we read, "[9] However, you are not in the flesh but in the Spirit, if indeed the Spirit of God dwells in you. But if anyone does not have the Spirit of Christ, he does not belong to Him. [10] If Christ is in you, though the body is dead because of sin, yet the spirit is alive because of righteousness. [11] But if the Spirit of Him who raised Jesus from the dead dwells in you, He who raised Christ Jesus from the dead will also give life to your mortal bodies through His Spirit who dwells in you." That "life" which God gives through His Spirit now dwelling in the person who believes the gospel of one's salvation is God's own righteous life, or righteousness, mentioned at verse 10. This life is eternal because two things are true here. One is that the person who believes now has The Holy Spirit, Who comes to indwell in one's spirit eternally, as we have seen at John 14:16,17 already. And two, this life which God imparts is eternal because God will never remove it from us, once given, but will continue to impart it to the believer eternally, that is, right on into eternity. Having said that, we also need to be aware of the fact that whenever one sins after salvation – and yes, one can still sin, due to still having a sinful nature inherited from Adam – then the flow of God's life is temporarily interrupted from flowing into our lives, since we have through our sin gone back to draw life from our sinful self, instead of from God. However, the moment our sin is confessed and forgiven by God, by the only means provided by God, noting 1 John 1:9 with 1 John 2:1,2, then the flow of God's righteous eternal life, or righteousness, is resumed, and we are back in fellowship with God, as God intends to be with all those who are part of His family.

What is very important to keep in mind as we conclude this present chapter is to note that what we have mentioned here, namely entering into a personal relationship with God, receiving the gift of The Holy Spirit, becoming a child of God by spiritual birth, receiving the forgiveness of sins, and also eternal life with God, that this is all done by God simultaneously the moment we believe the gospel, as a work of God's grace and power in us. In other words, these are not steps, taking place one after the other, but rather all of this takes place instantaneously, that is, all at once as wholly a work which God does the moment a person believes in God's precious Son, Jesus Christ. This also is an important truth to remember.

WHAT IS ONE BEING SAVED FROM AT SALVATION?

We have mentioned earlier in this section that salvation involved a deliverance, and now the question we want to look at in this present chapter is what is it that a person is being saved from, or delivered from, at the moment of one's salvation? And in order to answer this question, we now need to bring in some Biblical terms which God uses in His word to describe the salvation we receive from Him the moment we believe the gospel of His grace, relating to His precious Son, Jesus Christ, namely that He died for our sins, was buried, and was raised from the dead the third day.

And so, what we will do in this chapter then is to look at our God-wrought salvation, which He is outworking here on earth from the moment we become a child of His until the moment He takes us to Heaven, either through physical death, or through our part in the first resurrection. And what we now need to grasp is that this salvation is being viewed by God as being in three stages, with these three stages of our salvation being our justification, our sanctification, and our glorification.

Stage 1: Our justification

The first stage of our salvation is to be seen as being the very moment in time when God actually brings us into a personal relationship with Himself, which occurs the moment that we believe, as a work of God in us, that God's precious Son, Jesus Christ, died for one's sins, was buried, and then was raised from the dead the third day, thereby receiving in believing the forgiveness of one's sins and eternal life with God. We can therefore say that this first stage of our salvation is when God saves, or delivers us from the penalty of sin, which is death, since we have just come to personally believe, as a work of God in us, that when God's Son died on the cross, it was as my Substitute, to pay the penalty due my sins, which was death. And since in God's sight "all have sinned and fall short of the glory of God" (Romans 3:23), then God's Son is now seen as having died in my place on that cross.

And so we begin our new life with God by having all of our sins forgiven and being imputed His righteous life to live by, which becomes our righteousness, that is, the eternal life we now have with Him. As we see from Romans 8:30, "and these whom He predestined, He also called; and these whom He called, He also justified; and these whom He justified, He also glorified," that word "justified" speaks of now being in a state before God of being 'just as if we had never sinned,' due to all of our sins committed since the age of accountability having now been forgiven us, from the moment of our justification onward, which is the first stage of our God-wrought salvation! Our justification then is a work which God does in a moment of time to begin our salvation, and which never needs to be repeated.

Stage 2: Our sanctification

Then as to our sanctification, which is the second stage of our God-wrought salvation, we are now to see that it takes place between our justification and our glorification as children of God yet on earth. Whereas our justification is something which God does in a moment of time to begin our Christian life here on earth and is never repeated, and whereas our glorification is also something which God does in a moment of time to end our Christian life on earth and also never needs repeating, yet our sanctification is to now be seen as the process which God carries out between the time of our justification and the time of our glorification, whereby He sets us apart to do His will willingly on earth out of love for Him! Whereas we start our Christian life with God as those who have known only sin, God now sanctifies us, that is, sets us apart for Himself, that we may end our Christian life here on earth knowing only holiness, once our sinful nature is removed from us. And whereas we start our Christian life here on earth knowing only how to live out of our sinful nature, now God, in sanctification, that is, in this process of setting us apart for Himself, God teaches us how to live by His imparted righteousness, so that we may end our Christian life here on earth as conformed, as much as it is possible while in these bodies, to the image of His precious Son, Jesus Christ! And so that is why sanctification, as the second stage of our God-wrought salvation, can be regarded as when God saves, or delivers us from the power of sin, with 'sin' in view here being a reference to our sinful nature.

Stage 3: Our glorification

Then as already mentioned, our glorification is to be seen as the third stage of our God-wrought salvation, which is when our Christian life here on earth ends, when God brings all of His children into His Presence in Heaven. And as also already mentioned, our glorification is to be seen, as is true for our justification, as being an instantaneous act of God, whereby He now conforms us fully to the image of His precious Son, Jesus Christ, by removing the sinful nature from us and giving us new spiritual bodies to last forever in His Presence in Heaven. And that is why we can regard this third stage of our God-wrought salvation as being when God saves, or delivers us from the presence of sin, with the word 'sin' having reference to not only no longer having a sinful nature, but also refers to the fact that since we no longer have a sinful nature, then that means that we can never ever sin again! And that is prospect to look forward to indeed!

And what is very important to keep in mind here about the whole of our salvation is that all three stages are a work of God's grace and power alone, as we will see in a later chapter in this present section.

WHY IS IT SO IMPORTANT TO BE SAVED?

In this chapter, we want to go on and look at the very important question of why it is so important to be saved, both from our standpoint and from God's standpoint. Therefore, the present chapter will be divided into two sections, as follows:

1) Why it is so important for human beings to be saved from our standpoint

The answer may already be in the mind of most readers, since what is in view here is one's eternal destiny after the present life, which can only be in one of two places. In other words, when time ends and eternity begins, every human being born into this world physically in time will spend eternity either with God in Heaven, or eternity with Satan, the devil, in hell. What this means then is that since Heaven is God's home, then the only ones who go there are those who have come to know Him personally in salvation during the time of one's stay on earth. And of course this also means that those who do not come to know God personally in salvation during one's stay on earth in time will spend eternity in hell. Therefore, from the human standpoint, one's eternal wellbeing is at stake, for to be with God will be indescribable bliss, while to be in hell will be indescribable agony! That is why salvation is the most important gift which a human being can receive from God during one's stay on earth!

2) Why it is so important for human beings to be saved from God's standpoint

Then from God's standpoint, salvation of human beings is important because it fulfills the goal which He set out to accomplish when He created this world and the human beings to inhabit it in the first place. That is why we read at Genesis 1:26 that when God created human beings, it was in His own image, in His own likeness, in order that these human beings might come to know Him in a personal way and enjoy fellowship with Him during this present life on earth and then eternally with Him in Heaven. What this also means from God's standpoint is that for every human being saved, this means one less person will be under the dominion of Satan, the devil, eternally. Since

God's precious Son died for the sins of the whole of the human race (2 Corinthians 5:14,15; 1 John 2:1,2), then this also means that His death becomes effective and applicable to even more precious souls, each time one comes to personally know God in salvation.

WHO IS GOD'S PRIMARY FOCUS IN SALVATION?

What is also very important to consider and remember about salvation is that God has a primary focus, with the truth to be grasped here being given under the following two headings:

1) Although God's salvation through faith in His Son is only for human beings, yet it is for ALL human beings!

A truth which needs to be grasped relating to salvation, which has a bearing on evangelism, is that God's salvation is for all human beings on earth in time, bar none. In other words, there is no human being who is excluded from the gospel of God's grace. God's salvation is for all humankind, no matter what nationality, sex, skin color, language, race, religion, or age. God excludes no one, and neither should we, when sharing the gospel.

Another related truth here is that there is no one who is ever beyond God's ability to save. What this means is that if someone is still alive physically, then God is still able to save that person. Therefore, there is never anyone who is too sinful, or too sick, or too handicapped, so as to be beyond God's ability to save. Absolutely no one! And so when viewing any human being on earth, we should never look at a human being and conclude that 'there is no sense sharing the gospel with that person since that one is beyond saving.' Such thoughts are not of God and have no place in how we are to view people in evangelism.

2) God does not provide salvation for the angels who sinned against Him at the beginning of creation

Another sobering truth to be grasped here is that God was not under any obligation whatsoever to provide human beings with salvation, since God did not provide salvation for the angels who sinned against Him at the beginning of creation. When the archangel who later became Satan, the devil; when he sinned against God, there is about one third of the angels which sinned with him against God. And God does not provide salvation for any of these fallen angelic spirit beings. God has left them in their state of rebellion against Him, which means that they will spend all eternity in hell, away from God's Presence forever. And God could also have done the same with the human race, when we as a human race sinned against Him in Adam. But He did not, for which we can be eternally grateful, especially those human beings who do enter into the blessings of God's salvation in time!

SALVATION IS TO BE SEEN AS BEING WHOLLY A WORK OF GOD'S GRACE AND POWER ALONE!

The other day, I spent about four hours discussing our common faith with a Christian friend, and one of the things I shared with Him from my walk with God during the last 35 years is that we begin our salvation with God thinking that salvation was our own idea and that we are the one's who came to believe in God as a choice we made. Then as we grow spiritually, we come to realize that salvation is not just a work that we do, but still do not yet see that salvation as being wholly of God, and so the thought which occupies us for many years is that it is a cooperative effort, with God doing His part and we doing our part in salvation. Then it is only as God teaches us more of Himself and His ways, as we enter our more spiritually mature stage of our walk with God, that we then come to realize that salvation is wholly a work of God's grace and power alone!

And what needs to be grasped here in regards to the last statement above is that this truth is not a denominational truth, in terms of being true because it is the teaching of a particular system of theology found in some denominations on earth. But rather, this truth is true simply because it is the teaching of God's word! And here we would benefit in noting what God tells us at Ephesians 2:8-10, "[8] For by grace you have been saved through faith; and that not of yourselves, it is the gift of God; [9] not as a result of works, so that no one may boast. [10] For we are His workmanship, created in Christ Jesus for good works, which God prepared beforehand so that we would walk in them." There is a lot of truth being shared by God here, the most important from our present standpoint being what we read at verse 8 and 9, "For by grace you have been saved... it is the gift of God." In other words, it is by God's unmerited favor alone! And not only that, but what further seals the truth that salvation is wholly a work of God is the fact that we further read that it is a gift from God. A gift is not a gift if we earned it, but rather an obligation to be met. But God calls salvation a gift from Him to the human being who receives it, as one without any merit to receive it.

Then God seals the truth with yet another fact to be grasped, which is that salvation is by faith, that is, through one believing. This truth takes on added importance when we consider what God also says at Romans 4:16 in part, "For this reason it is by faith, in order that it may be in accordance with grace..." The principle which God brings forth here is to show that faith always excludes works, same as at Ephesians 2:8 and 9, so that whatever God is providing may be provided by grace, that is, by His unmerited favor alone. That is why God can add at Ephesians 2:10, "For we are His workmanship, created in Christ Jesus..." In other words, it is because of His grace and power alone in operation in us that we became a new creation of God in His precious Son, Jesus Christ, at the moment of our salvation!

This truth is so important to God that He yet amplifies it again at Romans 11, when He says at verses 5 and 6, "[5] In the same way then, there has also come to be at the present time a remnant according to God's gracious choice. [6] But if it is by grace, it is no longer on the basis of works, otherwise grace is no longer grace." God's grace always stands opposed to works which we do. What this means for our present discussion then is that we cannot be involved and God also involved in our salvation. Either it is all of us, or it is all of God. Since we have just seen that God has clearly stated that salvation is by His grace alone, then that means that human works are totally excluded. That is, we were not involved at all in our own salvation, but rather it was a work of God's grace and power alone!

And if anyone needs any other proof, we only need to look at the reality to be grasped from what God says about the whole of the human race in unbelief at Romans 3:10-12, "[10] as it is written, "There is none righteous, not even one; [11] There is none who understands, there is none who seeks for God; [12] all have turned aside, together they have become useless; there is none who does good, there is not even one." And as we bring this present chapter to a close, let us note a very important quote from God on this subject, namely that salvation is wholly a work of God's grace and power alone, by noting what God says to those who have become His children in salvation at Titus 3:3-

7, where we read, "[3] For we also once were foolish ourselves, disobedient, deceived, enslaved to various lusts and pleasures, spending our life in malice and envy, hateful, hating one another. [4] But when the kindness of God our Savior and His love for mankind appeared, [5] He saved us, not on the basis of deeds which we have done in righteousness, but according to His mercy, by the washing of regeneration and renewing by the Holy Spirit, [6] whom He poured out upon us richly through Jesus Christ our Savior, [7] so that being justified by His grace we would be made heirs according to the hope of eternal life." As we see at verses 4 and 5 here, "But... God... saved us... according to His mercy...being justified by His grace." Unless God intervenes and provides salvation, then one will indeed be going to a lost eternity after this life.

And as we close, let us give God the last word by noting 1 Corinthians 1:30,31, where He tells those who have come to know Him, "but by His doing you are in Christ Jesus, who became to us wisdom from God, and righteousness and sanctification, and redemption, [31] so that, just as it is written, "Let him who boasts, boast in the Lord." " Amen to that!

GOD'S SALVATION VIEWED IN THE LIGHT OF GOD'S SOVEREIGNTY AND GOD'S ELECTION

We have seen in the previous chapter that salvation is wholly a work of God's grace and power alone, which He does in time. What we need to do in this chapter then is relate this truth to two other truths which God has also made known in His word, namely that He is a Sovereign Being and that He does elect some for salvation, that is, that He does choose a people for Himself in eternity past and then does save them in time.

That God is Sovereign can be grasped from what He tells us at 1 Timothy 6:15, adding verses 14 and 16 for context, "[14] that you keep the commandment without stain or reproach until the appearing of our Lord Jesus Christ, [15] which He (God The Father) will bring about at the proper time — He who is the blessed and only Sovereign, the King of kings and Lord of lords, [16] who alone possesses immortality and dwells in unapproachable light, whom no man has seen or can see. To Him be honor and eternal dominion! Amen." What we need to grasp here is that the "He" in view at verse 15 is a reference to God The Father. It is He who is spoken of as being "The... only Sovereign...," Who is "The King of kings and Lord of lords... Who alone possesses immortality and dwells in unapproachable light, whom no man has seen or can see." The Father always remains invisible to the human eye in time, with The Son being the visible expression of God (Colossians 1:15). And for our present purpose here, we need to note that God is The only true Sovereign there is in existence for time and eternity!

When speaking of the word "sovereign" among men, we are making reference to those who rule with great authority over others. And what often goes along with the authority is the power to exercise that authority, although that is not always the case among humankind. One may have the authority, but lack the power to exercise it. However, when the word "Sovereign" is applied to God, then we are making reference to The only One Who has not only absolute authority to act, but also absolute power to act! God is not making an idle boast, but is rather simply setting forth the truth, when He declares at Isaiah 14:24, "The Lord of hosts has sworn saying, "Surely, just as I have intended so it has happened, and just as I have planned so it will stand," and again at Isaiah 46:10,11 in part, "[10] Declaring the end from the beginning, and from ancient times things which have not been done, saying, 'My purpose will be established, and I will accomplish all My good pleasure'; [11] ...truly I have spoken; truly I will bring it to pass. I have planned it, surely I will do it." As a believer walks with God and matures in the faith, one comes to see God's Sovereignty over all creation, that is, His absolute authority and power to act over all that exists. And here we can note what Job came to discover near the end of his own life as a believer, as one who had walked with God, noting what he exclaims at Job 42:2, adding v.1 for context, "[1] Then Job answered the Lord and said, [2] "I know that You can do all things, and that no purpose of Yours can be thwarted." "

Having now seen that God is Sovereign over all that exists in time and eternity, we then need to see that God is exercising His authority and power in accordance with a plan, which He has had from before creation took place and time began. If God were not working from a plan, then all of what occurs in all of creation in time would be utter chaos. And of course those in unbelief do not see God behind all that exists and so all such need to seek answers outside or apart from God for what happens in this world. However, that should never be the case for the child of God. We should be viewing this world and all which occurs from a Christian worldview, which has God on His throne and very much involved in even the very minute details of all which takes place moment by moment in His creation.

But what is God's plan of the ages, which He has had for all eternity and which He is outworking in time? There are a number of passages of Scripture where God has made this known to humankind, one being at Titus 2:14, where we read, "who gave Himself (that is, Christ Jesus) for us to redeem us from every lawless deed, and to purify for Himself a people for His own possession, zealous for good deeds." When God says here, "...to redeem us from every lawless deed, and to purify for Himself a people for His own possession, zealous for good deeds," we have God's purpose of the ages, which is to have a people, made up of human beings, who will willingly serve Him out of love for Him! And although that is God's purpose, we also need to note what God also said at Titus 2:14 here, namely "...to redeem us... and to purify for Himself..." In other words, God had to buy back from the slave market sinners who were willingly slaves to sin and only willing to serve self.

The words "redeem" here and the word "purify" speak of two works which God has to do before we become His children, and before we willingly serving Him out of love for Him. The work of redemption and purification God does begin at the moment of one's salvation, when God grants an unbelieving sinner the faith to believe in Him, noting again what we read at Colossians 1:12-14, "[12] giving thanks to the Father, who has qualified us to share in the inheritance of the saints in Light. [13] For He rescued us from the domain of darkness, and transferred us to the kingdom of His beloved Son, [14] in whom we have redemption, the forgiveness of sins." We need to notice here that this is a work which God must do, in terms of transferring us from the dominion of Satan, the devil, whom we were gladly serving unknowingly, in order to now be part of the Kingdom of His beloved Son, in order to now serve God knowingly and willingly out of love for Him, as those who have been redeemed by God and forgiven all of one's sins committed against God.

And let us also ever keep in mind that the only basis by which God can forgive guilty sinners and then grant eternal life with Himself is ever the death of His own precious Son for the sins committed by the human race in time - for the penalty for sin is death – followed by His burial and subsequent resurrection from the dead the third day, for it is through His Son as ever alive that God imparts those who believe in Him His eternal life to live by. This we also see from what God says above at Titus 2:14, Who, when speaking of His precious Son, Jesus Christ, says of Him, "Who gave Himself for us to redeem us..." Apart from the death, burial, and resurrection from the dead of His own precious Son on behalf of a sinful human race, God has no basis for forgiving guilty sinners and granting eternal life with Himself. Therefore, that is God's plan of the ages, to save a people for Himself out of a human race lost in sin, who will now serve Him willingly out of love for Him, doing that saving of a people for Himself on the basis of the death, burial, and resurrection from the dead of His own precious Son, Jesus Christ.

The truth to be realized here is that unless God is at work in the salvation of precious souls, as a work of His grace and power, then no one can be saved! And in this regard, we note what God tells us at Psalm 127:1, "Unless the Lord builds the house, they labor in vain who build it..." Likewise in the life of His precious Son while here on earth at His first coming from Heaven to earth, He did say to His disciples what we read at John 6:44,65 regarding the salvation of precious souls, "[44] No one can come to Me unless the Father who sent Me draws him; and I will raise him up on the last day... [65] And He was saying, "For this reason I have said to you, that no one can come to Me unless it has been granted him from the Father." Likewise, we note that the apostle Peter was mindful of the sovereignty of God in salvation as he preached at Jerusalem, noting what we read at Acts 2:39, "For the promise is for you and your children and for all who are far off, as many as the Lord our God will call to Himself." And we can also be sure that the apostle Paul and Barnabas were not ignorant of this important truth either, for we note what Luke was led of God to record at Acts 13:48 during the time that Paul and Barnabas preached at Psidian Antioch, "When the Gentiles heard this, they began rejoicing and glorifying the word of the Lord; and as many as had been appointed to eternal life believed."

Therefore, how important that we ever keep in mind, as God's people now on earth involved in evangelism, that God is Sovereign in salvation, and precious souls will be saved only if it is His will and timing for them to be saved, in which case we can be sure that He will be at work and the gospel will be preached to the saving of precious souls by His precious Holy Spirit through the vessel He desires to use (1 Peter 1:12)). And here we can further note for instance what we also read at Acts 11:17,18, after the apostle Peter was led of God to preach to the Gentiles gathered at Cornelius' home, at which time all those gathered came to faith in God, "[17] Therefore if God gave to them the same gift as He gave to us also after believing in the Lord Jesus Christ, who was I that I could stand in God's way?" [18] When they heard this, they quieted down and glorified God, saying, "Well then, God has granted to the Gentiles also the repentance that leads to life." This same truth is also seen at Acts 11:20,21, where we read, "[20] But there were some of them, men of Cyprus and Cyrene, who came to Antioch and began speaking to the Greeks also, preaching the Lord Jesus. [21] And the hand of the Lord was with them, and a large number who believed turned to the Lord." And just as many people have been brought to a saving knowledge of God through faith in His precious Son as a work of His grace and power since the beginning of creation, so too is God similarly carrying out His work in our day in salvation in accordance with His grace and power in Sovereignty, noting here what God reveals to us at Romans 3:24, regarding what He has done for each of us in salvation, "being justified as a gift by His grace through the redemption which is in Christ Jesus..."

In now having seen that salvation is a work which God does in time by His grace and power alone, while exercising His Sovereignty as Sovereign over His own creation, and having also seen that God does so in accordance with an eternal plan that He is working from, we can now go further and see how election fits into this, since election is a work which God does in eternity past, before creation even took place, which is when time began. And two verses which we can begin with here to bring us into the subject of God's election is noting what God says at 2 Thessalonians 2:13,14, "[13] But we should always give thanks to God for you, brethren beloved by the Lord, because God has chosen you from the beginning for salvation through sanctification by the Spirit and faith in the truth. [14] It was for this He called you through our gospel, that you may gain the glory of our Lord Jesus Christ." What is very important to notice here is that God is writing to believers, and says to them, "God has chosen you from the beginning for salvation..." The word "chosen" here means 'to take for Oneself,' in terms of selecting, in the act of exercising a choice. And that choice being made by God is "for salvation," so that those chosen may believe in God and so come to know Him in a personal relationship, which is in time.

It is also important to realize here that the word "beginning" does not refer to the time of creation and the beginning of time here, but rather is referring to WHEN God actually made that choice, which was in eternity past and known only to God as to the exact moment. This is clear from what we read at Ephesians

1:4, looking at verses 3 to 6 for context, "[3] Blessed be the God and Father of our Lord Jesus Christ, who has blessed us with every spiritual blessing in the heavenly places in Christ, [4] just as He chose us in Him before the foundation of the world, that we would be holy and blameless before Him. In love [5] He predestined us to adoption as sons through Jesus Christ to Himself, according to the kind intention of His will, [6] to the praise of the glory of His grace, which He freely bestowed on us in the Beloved." As we see from verse 4 here, God made a choice from "before the foundation of the world," that is, before creation took place and time began to be recorded.

Another passage where God speaks of salvation in time as being a work of His, while also being seen as a work which He began in eternity past, is noting what He tells us at 2 Timothy 1:8-10, where we read, "[8] Therefore do not be ashamed of the testimony of our Lord or of me His prisoner, but join with me in suffering for the gospel according to the power of God, [9] who has saved us and called us with a holy calling, not according to our works, but according to His own purpose and grace which was granted us in Christ Jesus from all eternity, [10] but now has been revealed by the appearing of our Savior Christ Jesus, who abolished death and brought life and immortality to light through the gospel..." Here we have what God led the apostle Paul to say to Timothy, who had been raised of God as an evangelist. And especially noteworthy for our present purpose is focusing on verse 9, where we clearly see that it is God who calls one elect of Him to salvation, when the time has arrived for one to come to know God, also noting that God is only bringing to pass in time, as a work of His grace and power, what He had purposed from eternity. The words" from all eternity" here simply refer to what took place before creation took place and time began to be marked.

Yet other verses from God's word which we can note here in this matter of God choosing, or electing, some human beings for Himself from before creation took place and time began, and then saving these in time, is at Romans 8:29,30, where God discloses to us, "[29] For those whom He foreknew, He also predestined to become conformed to the image of His Son, so that He would be the firstborn among many brethren; [30] and these whom He predestined, He also called; and these whom He called, He also justified; and these whom He justified, He also glorified." The reference to "those whom He foreknew" here speaks of those whom God The Father chose in eternity past to be His in time through salvation, seeing again from verse 30 that all such, being predestined by God to be His, are called to Himself in time to believe the gospel of God's grace, and in believing are justified, that is, declared by God to be 'just as if one had never sinned' against God, since now one's sins committed against God in time are all forgiven and one is brought into the family of God through a spiritual birth by The Holy Spirit coming to indwell in one's spirit.

The word "predestined" at verse 5 also speaks of this act of God being done from before creation took place and time began, for what is in view here is when God made the choice for some to believe in Him in eternity past, but the realization of it, in terms of those chosen to actually believe in Him for salvation, only takes place in time. Those who were chosen of God to be His in eternity past are destined to come to faith in God after creation has taken place and time has begun to be kept. All those predestined by God for salvation in eternity past will be saved in time, bar none.

But one question which one might legitimately ask here is: But why did God have to elect, or choose, some in eternity past for salvation in time? And the answer is because of the entrance of sin in the human race. The moment the parents of the whole human race, Adam and Eve, sinned against God, they not only became sinners before a Holy God by that one act of sin, but they became sinners by nature! What that meant is that sin corrupted the whole of their nature, so that now all their actions, words, and thoughts were only evil all the time in Gods sight, because now coming from a sinful self which had been corrupted by sin. And that sinful nature was then passed on to their offspring through the male, so that sin then spread to the whole human race. In other words, the whole human race comes to personally know sin at the age of accountability, which is when a child first learns good and evil, and freely chooses the evil due to having a sinful nature inherited at birth, now becoming personally accountable to God for one's sin against

Him. And since the consequence of sin is death, then death also spread to the whole human race through sin, which is why God is stating a very far reaching truth when He says at Romans 3:23, "for all have sinned and fall short of the glory of God," and again at Romans 5:12, "Therefore, just as through one man (Adam) sin entered into the world, and death through sin, and so death spread to all men, because all sinned" (at the age of accountability).

And so that is why God had to elect, or choose some human beings for Himself in eternity past to believe in Him in time, for He knew before creation even took place and time began that when sin did enter the whole of the human race, then what God says in part at Isaiah 53:6 would be true, "All of us like sheep have gone astray, each of us has turned to his own way..." Then as a consequence of the whole human race having gone astray and far from God is what God further says at Romans 3:10 to 12, where we read this sobering statement, which is God's assessment of the human race after it had gone astray from Him due to sin, "[10] There is none righteous, not even one; [11] there is none who understands, there is none who seeks for God; [12] all have turned aside, together they have become useless; there is none who does good, there is not even one." So apart from God's intervention, there never would have been anyone who ever would have believed in God in time, so that the world could have gone on for an eternity and God's original plan of having a people for Himself, willingly serving Him out of love for Him would never have been realized! And so that is why God did elect, or choose some for Himself before creation took place and time began, and then does bring each so chosen to a personal relationship with Himself in salvation in time, because otherwise none would ever be saved, that is, would ever come to know Him!

Another legitimate question which one might ask here is: But why would God allow sin, if He knew that the whole of the human race would go astray from Him as a consequence, resulting in none ever believing in Him? And the answer to that question is that God being God knew that apart from allowing sin, God could never be fully known as He really is, in all His attributes. This may sound like an enigmatic statement, until we

72

come to realize for instance that one of God's attributes is that He is good, but the reality is that what is good cannot be known apart from knowing what evil is, which is the opposite of good. And one cannot know what evil is in order to know what good is without sin having been allowed by God! For it is only in knowing the opposite that we come to know the other. For instance, God is love (1 John 4:8,16), but God cannot be known as such unless one first comes to know what the opposite of love is, which is hatred. God was looking for human beings to believe in Him and serve Him willingly out of love for Him, and not robots who were programmed by God in only knowing one thing, but rather as human beings who were fully aware, who knew what evil was, so that they might appreciate God as He fully is, after having come to know Him in salvation!

What has just been said above is also true in nature. We can only appreciate a beautiful sunny day simply because we have come to know and experience the contrasting cloudy and rainy days. If God had created a world with just sunny days, as He could have, we would not be appreciating a sunny day today as we now do in having the contrast. God's wisdom and vast knowledge can be seen throughout nature, so that one never hears of a person criticizing God for what He has done in nature, and yet we as but finite created beings are so quick to criticize God or ascribe some unfairness to God in regards to His election of some to salvation, while leaving the rest to their free choice of rejecting Him while on earth.

And while mentioning free choice here, we need to realize that man's free choice, for both believers and unbelievers alike, operates only within God's Sovereign control over all that exists in creation and for all time and eternity. What this means in relation to election is that when God elected some to salvation in eternity past, He did so knowing that ALL human beings would be freely going to a lost eternity away from Him, bar none, unless He intervened. It was an act of God's mercy, grace, and love to intervene. He did not have to intervene, since He did not intervene for the angels which went astray from Him shortly after their creation. But those who are chosen of God for salvation in time are praising God for that intervention from the moment that God brings a person to faith in Himself. Those who are not chosen are simply left in their hatred of God. I was once speaking to a man in his midforties about his eternal destiny, and his answer was, "Well, I want to be in hell, for that is where all my friends will be." The sobering truth is that those who perish are simply being left to their free choice by God. Now mind you, unbelievers will never know what God is like, never having come to know God in a personal relationship, so that when they enter hell for eternity, the only difference from now is that they will have a body which lasts forever and they will be in conscious torment, compared to what they are experiencing today.

So let us never charge God with unfairness in regards to His election of some to salvation, out of all who were gladly rejecting Him, for what ever needs to be remembered is that God could not provide that salvation for any human beings until His own precious Son had suffered and died for the sins of the whole human race. If one wants to find something unfair, then say that it was unfair for God's Son to have to suffer and die for the sins of the whole human race, that God may have a basis to even save some in time, and then in the end God might have a people serving Him willingly out of love for Him. In my experience, those who criticize God's election of some for salvation are those who have never spent enough time with God in prayer for Him to show them the truth of that doctrine.

So may we be granted God's grace, encouragement, and strength to persevere in God's work, as we wait on God to bring in precious souls through us, and even when we do not see immediate fruit, knowing that God is Sovereign in salvation, and apart from Him we cannot do anything, noting here John 15:16, where we read, "You did not choose Me but I chose you, and appointed you that you would go and bear fruit, and that your fruit would remain, so that whatever you ask of the Father in My name He may give to you." For what needs to be grasped here, which is the first topic we deal with in the next section on evangelism, is that evangelism is also a work which God does! And another truth closely related to this one is that God saves us in order that we might willingly serve Him out of love for Him, and so for the whole of Christian lives, after coming to know God in salvation, we are but vessels in His Hands for Him to use

74

to accomplish His will on earth. And part of His will is to bring to salvation in time to those who are chosen of Him for Himself in eternity past. Also, part of that will is to use us Who know Him as vessels in His Hands to reach those who are elect, but who as yet do not know Him. But more on this vital subject in the next section, which is specifically on this topic of evangelism.

IF GOD DID NOT EVANGELIZE,

THEN NO ONE WOULD EVER BE SAVED!

SECTION THREE

EVANGELISM AS GOD INTENDED

EVANGELISM IS WHAT GOD DOES BEST, WHICH IS WHY WE NEED TO SEE OURSELVES AS SIMPLY THE VESSESLS HE DELIGHTS TO USE!

We closed the last section by saying that evangelism, like everything else associated with our salvation, both before and after, is a work which God does in time, with those who know Him simply being vessels in His Hands to accomplish the task. What we now need to see in this section, and this chapter in particular, is the truth of this, as being something which God Himself says in His word. For a truth is only a truth when God has stated it in His word, the Bible.

So now let us see from God's word that evangelism is what God does best, with our simply seeing ourselves, as God's children yet on earth, as vessels He delights to use in that task. And one passage we can begin with is looking at 2 Corinthians 5:14 to 6:2, where God speaks of the salvation of precious souls in time in the context of that being His work with the involvement of believers, noting now what we there read, "[5:14] For the love of Christ controls us, having concluded this, that one died for all, therefore all died; [15] and He died for all, so that they who live might no longer live for themselves, but for Him who died and rose again on their behalf. [16] Therefore from now on we recognize no one according to the flesh; even though we have known Christ according to the flesh, yet now we know Him in this way no longer. [17] Therefore if anyone is in Christ, he is a new creature; the old things passed away; behold, new things have come. [18] Now all these things are from God, who reconciled us to Himself through Christ and gave us the ministry of reconciliation, [19] namely, that God was in Christ reconciling the world to Himself, not counting their trespasses against them, and He has committed to us the word of reconciliation. [20] Therefore, we are ambassadors for Christ, as though God were making an appeal through us; we beg you on behalf of Christ, be reconciled to God. [21] He made Him who knew no sin to be sin on our behalf, so that we might become the righteousness of God in Him. [6:1] And working together *with Him*, we also urge you not to receive the grace of God in vain — [2] for He says, "At the acceptable time I listened to you, and on the day of

81

salvation I helped you." Behold, now is "the acceptable time," behold, now is "the day of salvation." "

To begin with, let us notice at verse 18 and 19 that salvation is a work which God does, when He says, "Now all these things are from God, who reconciled us to Himself through Christ... namely, that God was in Christ reconciling the world to Himself, not counting their trespasses against them." And secondly, let us then notice that God involves us as believers in that work of salvation, which He does, noting what we read from verse 18 to 20, "God, who... gave us the ministry of reconciliation... and He has committed to us the word of reconciliation. Therefore, we are ambassadors for Christ, as though God were making an appeal through us; we beg you on behalf of Christ, be reconciled to God." Notice especially that we are to be so involved with God in that work of salvation, which He is doing, that He says that it is "as though God were making an appeal through us." What this means is that when we are sharing the gospel with someone, it is actually God Who is at work in us and through us, not only creating the opportunity and not only leading us to the words to say, but after we have shared the truth regarding His precious Son, it is also God who works in the heart of the hearer to believe the gospel that was just shared and in believing to be saved, in terms of now becoming a child of God, with The Holy Spirit coming to indwell, while cleansing one of all sins ever committed against God in one's life and also now imparting God's life for one to live by, as now being a child of God on earth. That what has just been shared is so can be grasped from what God says to us at 1 Peter 1:12, where we read, "It was revealed to them that they were not serving themselves, but you, in these things which now have been announced to you through those who preached the gospel to you by the Holy Spirit sent from heaven — things into which angels long to look," and also at John 6:63, where God The Father tells us through His precious Son, "It is the Spirit who gives life; the flesh profits nothing; the words that I have spoken to you are spirit and are life."

What also needs to be noticed from the passage in 2 Corinthians 5:14 to 6:2 quoted above is that the only time that God cannot use us as vessels for Him to save precious souls through us is when we are not available to God, which is why God says here at verse 20, "we beg you on behalf of Christ, be reconciled to God." The word "reconciled" here speaks of one going from a state of enmity toward God to one of fellowship with God. When used in the context of unbelievers, the word is used of the reconciliation which God brings about in salvation as a work of His grace toward a sinner on the basis of the death of His own Son, Jesus Christ, having already paid the penalty due sin, which is death, on behalf of all sinners of time. But what needs to be noticed here is that at verse 20 the word "reconciled" is actually used in the context of believers, which means that the only time that God cannot use us as vessels in His work of evangelism is when we are not walking with Him. And the only time that we are not walking with God is when there is known unconfessed sins in our lives. Therefore, when God says "be reconciled to God" here, He is meaning that His child needs to do some self-examination to see what it is in one's life that is preventing one from being a vessel in God's Hands in this vital work which God is doing, namely evangelizing the world. And so let us ensure that we are walking with God moment by moment so that we might be vessels in His Hands which He can use to do the work which is so close to His own heart. God knows that He yet has precious souls to bring in into His family and He wants to use those who are already His as vessels in His Hands to bring that about. Let us not be like the older son in the parable of the two sons at Luke 15, where the older son did not share the father's heart toward his own.

What also needs to be noticed from the passage at 2 Corinthians 5:14 to 6:2 is that God uses the death of His Son as the motivating factor to move us to be involved with God in the work which He is doing of evangelizing the lost of this world, so as to bring into His family those who are chosen of Him for salvation from before the foundation of the world. And here we need to notice what God says at verses 14,15 and 21, where we read, "[14] For the love of Christ controls us, having concluded this, that one died for all, therefore all died; [15] and He died for all, so that they who live might no longer live for themselves, but for Him who died and rose again on their behalf... [21] He made Him who knew no sin to be sin on our behalf, so that we might become the righteousness of God in Him." The word "controls" at verse 14 here speaks of the effect the love of Christ should have on us, when we are walking with God with no known unconfessed sins in our lives. And what God means here by "the love of Christ" is not that it is our love for Christ being what controls us, but rather the love which God's precious Son, Jesus Christ, showed us when He died in our place, as our Substitute, at the cross of Calvary, paying the penalty of death due our sins! In other words, the motivating factor for one no longer living for self but for God after salvation is the death of God's own Son on our behalf. Three times here, namely in verses 14,15, and 21, God brings up the death of His precious Son, because God's love was shown to all human beings in that death, which should motivate those whom God saves to no longer live on earth for one's own will, but rather for God's will, which in this passage is focused on the salvation of precious souls, namely the bringing in through believers those who are elect of God, but not yet saved.

One verse we can note here in relation to what has just been said is 1 John 3:16, where we read, "We know love by this, that He laid down His life for us; and we ought to lay down our lives for the brethren." At John 3:16, we have the love of God for us being in focus when He gave His own precious Son to die in our place so that we might never perish, but have eternal life with God; but at 1 John 3:16, the focus is on the love of The Son of God for us, when He gave Himself a ransom in payment for our sins. It is this love which God wants to see grip us so as to move us to be vessels in His Hands, through whom He can bring in now in time those chosen of Him in eternity past. If this love is not motivating us now, then let us ask God to bring us to the place where it does, so that we might share God's heart, in terms of being where God is working.

Let us remember what God's Son had to tell the twelve one day, whom He was training to carry on the ministry once He had returned to Heaven, noting what we read at John 4:35, "Do you not say, 'There are yet four months, and then comes the harvest'? Behold, I say to you, lift up your eyes and look on the fields, that they are white for harvest." What was true then is still true today, namely that the fields are white for harvest. And the problem then is still the problem now, noting what God's precious Son also said to the disciples at Matthew 9:37,38, "[37] Then He said to His disciples, "The harvest is plentiful, but the workers are few. [38] Therefore beseech the Lord of the harvest to send out workers into His harvest." " And for our present purpose here, please also notice from verse 38 that "The Lord of the harvest" is God" and also that it is the bringing in of "His harvest" that we are all working together for as vessels in God's Hands. That is why God goes on to encourage us in the work of evangelism at 2 Corinthians 6:1,2 by saying, "[1] And working together *with Him*, we also urge you not to receive the grace of God in vain — [2] for He says, "At the acceptable time I listened to you, and on the day of salvation I helped you." Behold, now is "the acceptable time," behold, now is "the day of salvation." As God says here, "now is the day of salvation," for the door has not yet closed in the present age in which we are living, which means that there are yet precious souls to be brought into God's family. Let us indeed not be recipient's of God's grace in vain, but rather let us all be willing vessels in God's Hands, which He can use to share our faith with those whom God leads us to or places across our path, that they too might enjoy the blessing of salvation. Let us bring this important chapter to a close by noting what the apostle Paul was led of God to say at 2 Timothy 2:10 on this very matter we have been discussing here, "For this reason I endure all things for the sake of those who are chosen, so that they also may obtain the salvation which is in Christ Jesus and with it eternal glory."

In the next chapter, we will be looking at the example of God's own precious Son, Jesus Christ, Who at His first coming from Heaven to earth was the Pattern for us which The Father put forth for us to follow in this vital matter of evangelizing the lost of this world.

WE ARE TO SEE THAT GOD PUT FORTH HIS OWN SON AS THE PATTERN FOR US IN THIS MATTER OF EVANGELISM

What we want to do in this chapter is to see that God's own precious Son, Jesus Christ, was Himself a vessel in His Father's Hands the whole time while here on earth at His first coming from heaven to earth, being put forth as a Pattern for us, as God's children yet on earth. And to see this, we need to begin at the time God's eternal Son did take on our humanity, doing so in the innocence of Adam and as born of a virgin so as not to incur our sinful nature, noting what we read at Hebrews 10:5-7, "[5] Therefore, when He comes into the world, He says, "Sacrifice and offering You have not desired, but a body You have prepared for Me; [6] in whole burnt offerings and sacrifices for sin You have taken no pleasure. [7] Then I said, 'Behold, I have come (In the scroll of the book it is written of Me) To do Your will, O God.' "

Therefore, we are to see that from the very moment God's Son came from Heaven to earth to partake of our humanity, in the innocence of Adam as first created, and until He was taken up to Heaven again after His death for our sins, His burial, and His resurrection from the dead, God's precious Son, Jesus Christ, ever lived as a vessel in His Father's Hands, willingly doing His Father's will out of love for Him, doing so as a Pattern for us. And we would be helped here in noting what God's Son also disclosed at John 6:38 while carrying out His ministry on earth, "For I have come down from heaven, not to do My own will, but the will of Him who sent Me." Since God's precious Son never sinned, ever living in an unbroken relationship with His precious Father, He was not in need of salvation after He came from Heaven to earth. His focus on the doing of His precious Father's will here was but to leave us a Pattern, as those who come to know God in a personal relationship at salvation!

And when the time came for God's Son to go to the cross, be buried, and then rise from the dead the third day, and before returning to Heaven again forty days later, He could look back at His thirty-three and a half years on earth and say to His Father what we read at John 17:4, "I glorified You on the earth, having accomplished the work which You have given Me to do." And so we see that during His whole time on earth, God's precious Son, Jesus Christ, did nothing but His Father's will, culminating with His death for us at the cross. And please notice that at Philippians 2:5-8, God The Father uses the Pattern which His precious Son left us to encourage us, who know Him in salvation, to do likewise, noting what God there says to us (in the King James version in this instance only), "[5] Let this mind be in you, which was also in Christ Jesus: [6] Who, being in the form of God (that is, in the very nature of), thought it not robbery to be equal with God: [7] But made himself of no reputation, and took upon him the form of a servant (that is, in the very nature of), and was made in the likeness of men: [8] And being found in fashion as a man (after He took on our humanity), he humbled himself, and became obedient unto death, even the death of the cross."

And then for the purpose of this present chapter, we are also to see that part of the will of God The Father for His precious Son, Jesus Christ, while on earth as a Pattern for us, was for The Son to be a willing vessel in His Father's Hands for bringing precious souls to salvation, whom God had predestined in eternity past to be saved in time. The one key passage which will serve our purpose here will be to look at John 4, where The Father works through His precious Son as a willing vessel in His Hands to bring first a Samaritan woman to Himself in salvation, and then many other Samaritans from the city in which she lived. We will not be looking at every verse from verses 3 to 42 here, where this encounter takes place, but rather only focusing on certain verses to serve our present purpose. Therefore, let us look at this true story of what did happen in the life of God's Son while on earth and let us learn all which God wants us to learn from His Son as our Pattern for being a willing vessel in His precious Father's Hands in this matter of evangelism.

First then, we note at John 4:3 to 6 that we have the background for this true story, which we need to be aware of, there reading, "[3] He left Judea and went away again into Galilee. [4] And He had to pass through Samaria. [5] So He came to a city of Samaria called Sychar, near the parcel of ground that Jacob gave to his son Joseph; [6] and Jacob's well was there. So Jesus, being wearied from His journey, was sitting thus by the well. It was about the sixth hour." The first key truth to notice here is what we are told at verse 4, namely that "He had to pass through Samaria." This does not mean anything to us until we realize that Jews did not associate with the Samaritans, which were the foreign people the king of Assyria brought to Samaria after the exile of the Northern Kingdom of Israel to Assyria in 722 BC, which account is told us at 2 Kings 17:6 and 24. And since that time the Jews would bypass Samaria when traveling from Judea to Galilee, as we read at verse 3, and similarly for the return route, crossing over the Jordan to travel on the east side of the Jordan river. Therefore, what we read at verse 4, in terms of God's precious Son having "to pass through Samaria," introduces us to the purpose of God for why His Son had to pass through Samaria that day, which was because God The Father had a Divine encounter that day and the next day in Samaria, where precious souls were to come to know God in a personal relationship, souls which had been chosen of God for salvation in eternity past, and whose time had now come for them to come to know God.

Then still keeping with the background information which we need to know in order to understand this true story, we are further told at verses 7 to 9, "[7] There came a woman of Samaria to draw water. Jesus said to her, "Give Me a drink." [8] For His disciples had gone away into the city to buy food. [9] Therefore the Samaritan woman said to Him, "How is it that You, being a Jew, ask me for a drink since I am a Samaritan woman?" (For Jews have no dealings with Samaritans.)" Let us notice here that God's Son knew that this was a Divine encounter on His calendar, one which was prepared by His precious Father for Him to accomplish, as a willing vessel in His Father's Hands. Therefore, The Son did not question His going to Samaria here, nor did He question His having to speak to Samaritans, in order for His precious Father's will to be done! And let us also notice that the twelve are not with God's precious Son in this encounter with this woman, for as was noted in my sixth book, titled "Deeper Truths Of The Christian Life," the twelve are totally unaware of the Divine encounter taking place here, as we will see in a moment.

Then because this Divine encounter is of God and for the purpose of this Samaritan coming to faith in God through His Son, then we see from the interchange taking place between John 4:10-30 that this is indeed what happens. And since the twelve had gone to the city of the Samaritans to buy food, we now see them offer some to God's precious Son, but are surprised and likely somewhat perplexed by His answer, noting verses 31 to 38 here, "[31] Meanwhile the disciples were urging Him, saying, "Rabbi, eat." [32] But He said to them, "I have food to eat that you do not know about." [33] So the disciples were saying to one another, "No one brought Him anything to eat, did he?" [34] Jesus said to them, "My food is to do the will of Him who sent Me and to accomplish His work. [35] Do you not say, 'There are yet four months, and then comes the harvest'? Behold, I say to you, lift up your eyes and look on the fields, that they are white for harvest. [36] Already he who reaps is receiving wages and is gathering fruit for life eternal; so that he who sows and he who reaps may rejoice together. [37] For in this case the saying is true, 'One sows and another reaps.' [38] "I sent you to reap that for which you have not labored; others have labored and you have entered into their labor." As we see at verses 32 and 34 here, God's Son is being urged by His disciples to take physical food, but in doing God's will, this required The Son to partake of spiritual food, which He did not want to set aside until all His Father had Him there for had been accomplished, which we need to remember was simply as a vessel in His precious Father's Hands. This is clear from a later statement which The Son was to make to the same disciples at John 14:10, where we read, "Do you not believe that I am in the Father, and the Father is in Me? The words that I say to you I do not speak on My own initiative, but the Father abiding in Me does His works."

Then as we further see at John 4:35 to 38 above, God's Son has to teach the disciples and us the very important truth that as God's children, we are in God's harvest field, which is ripe for the picking, with the only thing standing in our way of being vessels in God's Hands for the work which He is doing is our availability to God! These disciples were simply not available to God, and therefore were not being used by God to reach precious souls in Samaria, with God The Father having to use

90

only His precious Son as prepared and available to Him. This is what we will now look at in the next chapter and following, namely being prepared and available vessels for God to use in evangelism, in order to be effective vessels in God's Hands for the salvation of precious souls.

THE EFFECTIVENESS OF THE VESSEL DEPENDS ON THE VESSEL BEING PREPARED AND AVAILABLE TO GOD

When we invite people over for a meal, we do not use unwashed plates, cups, and cutlery from the dishwasher, but rather, we use what has been washed and is just waiting in the cupboard to be used for the meal. The same is true if we own a business and are looking for workers. We do not look for shady characters, but ensure we hire the best possible workers we can, for the success of the business will depend on it. And so when it comes to God using His own children yet on earth as vessels in His Hands to reach the unsaved which He wants to also bring into His family, He is particular about the vessels which He wants to use in that work. This is therefore what we will look at in this chapter, namely being prepared and available vessels so as to be effectively used by God in this work of evangelism leading to the salvation of precious souls He desires to reach through us.

One good passage of God's word where He speaks to us about this very matter is at 2 Timothy 2:19-21, where He says to us, "[19] Nevertheless, the firm foundation of God stands, having this seal, "The Lord knows those who are His," and, "Everyone who names the name of the Lord is to abstain from wickedness." [20] Now in a large house there are not only gold and silver vessels, but also vessels of wood and of earthenware, and some to honor and some to dishonor. [21] Therefore, if anyone cleanses himself from these things, he will be a vessel for honor, sanctified, useful to the Master, prepared for every good work." God speaks here of the preparedness and availability of those who are His yet on earth, which includes this task of evangelism. And the key requirement for the preparedness of the vessel here, which is the believer, is "if anyone cleanses himself..." What God has in view here is having a vessel in which there are no known unconfessed sins in one's life.

Then please also note that God goes on to say that such a clean vessel is automatically "a vessel for honor, sanctified (that is, set apart), useful to the Master (Who is God), prepared for every good work" (which includes evangelism). Therefore, as children of God yet on earth, we are to continually ensure that we are cleansed vessels for Him to use, by having no known unconfessed sins in our lives. If there is any known unconfessed sins in our lives, then God's righteous life, which God's word refers to as 'His righteousness,' cannot flow from God to us for us to live by while in these bodies as now God's children. The only remedy and confessional provided by God for His child who has sinned after salvation is 1 John 1:9, where God says, "If we confess our sins, He is faithful and righteous to forgive us our sins and to cleanse us from all unrighteousness." Since God's precious Son, Jesus Christ, has already died to pay the penalty for our sins – past, present, and future – then God has the basis for ever continually forgiving His child for any sin committed after salvation.

What the foregoing means then is that the only thing which will prevent us from being prepared, available, and effective vessels in God's Hands in this work of evangelism is sin in us! Remove the sin through confession to God and one is automatically a vessel ready for God's use, as we see at verse 21. This matter of dealing with known unconfessed sins in our lives God first leaves with us, and when we are unwilling to deal with it, then God simply has to intervene, which the end result being simply to takes us home, noting for instance what we read at 1 Corinthians 11:27-32, where God warns all those who are His and yet on earth, "[27] Therefore whoever eats the bread or drinks the cup of the Lord in an unworthy manner, shall be guilty of the body and the blood of the Lord. [28] But a man must examine himself, and in so doing he is to eat of the bread and drink of the cup. [29] For he who eats and drinks, eats and drinks judgment to himself if he does not judge the body rightly. [30] For this reason many among you are weak and sick, and a number sleep. [31] But if we judged ourselves rightly, we would not be judged. [32] But when we are judged, we are disciplined by the Lord so that we will not be condemned along with the world." In the passage just quoted, God has here in view the partaking of The Lord's Supper while having known unconfessed sins in one's life, which is a serious matter in God's sight, with the result being a warning to the child of God, first in the words "weak and sick," followed by physical death, as we see at verse 30 in the words "and a number sleep," when there is no confession of known unconfessed sin. As we see from verse 31, to avoid God's judgment of us, then we need to judge ourselves, in terms of confessing to Him any known unconfessed sins in our lives before partaking of The Lord's Supper. Sin in one's life as a child of God is serious business, which God does not take lightly, especially when we are slow or unwilling to deal with our sin. Then He has to step in and discipline us, as we see at verse 32.

As we close this chapter, think about what a happy moment it was in your life, if a parent, when a child was born into your family. Now just imagine the joy which God has, which includes all the angels in Heaven (Luke 15:7,10), when a human being comes to know God in a personal relationship at salvation, thereby being born spiritually into God's family. What this means then is that when we are cleansed and available vessels in God's Hands, we are not just vessels which God can then use effectively to reach precious souls in evangelism, but we are actually sharing in God's joy of seeing precious souls come to know Him in salvation. There is no greater joy possible for a human being than to personally know God in salvation, with the next best thing being involved with God in that work of seeing others likewise enter into that joy of personally knowing God! We are growing in spiritual maturity when we come to realize that God saved us by His grace and power alone that we might willingly serve Him out of love for Him after salvation!

EVANGELISM VIEWED IN LIGHT OF GOD'S SOVEREIGNTY IN ELECTION

What we want to do in this present chapter is deal with the statement which we sometimes hear, which goes something like this: 'Since all those chosen of God for salvation in eternity past will all come to know God at some point in time before physical death, then what is the point of our doing evangelism, since God will bring all these people to faith in Himself anyway?' Hopefully, all who have read the book so far would be able to answer this statement. And the first answer that one can give the person making such a statement is that it is partly true, in that God has indeed chosen some in eternity past for salvation in time, and all those so chosen will indeed come to know God in a personal relationship in time before physical death, bar none. However, what is not true in the statement is saying, 'then what is the point of our doing evangelism?' For what the person saying this misses is the truth that God has determined that He would do this work of evangelism through those who are already part of His family on earth! That this is so was seen for instance in the passage at 2 Corinthians 5:14 to 6:2, which we have looked at already and where we have seen that God desires ALL believers after salvation to be vessels in His Hands to reach others with the gospel, that they too might become children of God in salvation!

What needs to be grasped here is that one of the greatest privileges which God grants human beings on earth is to procreate after one's kind. In other words, for a man to take a wife, and within the loving confines of the married relationship, to have children together. And many humans, including many believers, have come to know the great joy involved in this! What we often do not realize as God's children after salvation is that God also desires those who have come to Him in salvation to also procreate spiritually after salvation, so as to not only personally know the joy of seeing someone be born spiritually in God's family, but of also sharing that joy with God, with Whom we have been involved in that work. So God has determined that we be involved with Him in that work of evangelism, as willing vessels in His Hands, continually cleansed and available, so that He can use us to reach others with the gospel, so that we might then share in God's joy of seeing these precious souls come to know God. This is a privilege which God grants ALL His children yet on earth after salvation.

Therefore, to not be involved with God in evangelism is simply in effect saying to God, 'I am not available for You to use.' Any one who is not a willing vessel in God's Hands for the purpose of reaching those whom God would like to bring to Himself in salvation is yet ignorant of the purpose for which one was saved by God. May God open our eyes to see clearly in these last days of the present age. May all of us personally experience the great joy there is not only being parents to children physically, but may we all also experience the great joy of being parents to children spiritually as well!

GOD SAVES EVERY PERSON IN TIME IN EXACTLY THE SAME WAY, THROUGH BELIEVING IN HIS PRECIOUS SON, CENTERED ON HIS DEATH FOR OUR SINS, HIS BURIAL, AND HIS RESURRECTION FROM THE DEAD!

SECTION FOUR

THE ROLE OF THE EVANGELIST

THE RELATION BETWEEN AN APOSTLE AND AN EVANGELIST

In this chapter, we will look at what the relation is between an apostle and an evangelist. For without fail, this is one area where believers all over the world have a knowledge gap. For one thing, few believers ever bother to find out what the relation is between these two servants of God, whom God has given as gifts to His church. On the one hand, not too many believers are ever an apostle or an evangelist in time. And on the other hand, it seems that there are more important questions to occupy believers than to give much thought to the relation between an apostle and an evangelist. However, since this is a book dealing with evangelism as God intended, then we cannot avoid bringing up this subject in order to deal with it, as we now do in this chapter. First, then, we will look at what God says about an apostle. Why? Because the critical truth which will be shared in this chapter is that the apostle is only for the foundation of the church, so that from then on, until the end of the church age, the apostle is replaced by the evangelist. Therefore, much of what God says about apostles, applies also to evangelists, as we will see.

a) An apostle: The necessary background to help our understanding

The best approach here is to start with what God says in His word regarding apostles, looking first at the necessary background before going on to add additional truth as we go on. And so we note that the first occurrence of the word in Scripture is at Matthew 10:2, where we will look at verses 1 to 5 (in part) for context, "[1] Jesus summoned His twelve disciples and gave them authority over unclean spirits, to cast them out, and to heal every kind of disease and every kind of sickness. [2] Now the names of the twelve apostles are these: The first, Simon, who is called Peter, and Andrew his brother; and James the son of Zebedee, and John his brother; [3] Philip and Bartholomew; Thomas and Matthew the tax collector; James the son of Alphaeus, and Thaddaeus; [4] Simon the Zealot, and Judas Iscariot, the one who betrayed Him. [5] These twelve Jesus sent out after instructing them:..." What we are to learn from this passage is that God's precious Son, Jesus Christ, is here seen appointing twelve of His disciples as apostles, as those who were to be "sent out" after being instructed by Him. The word "apostles" at verse 2, which is the word "apostolos" in the original Greek language of the New Testament, refers to "one sent forth." We also note from verse 1 that these original twelve apostles had been given authority by God to heal every kind of disease and sickness, and also given the authority to cast out demons from those who were demon-possessed. Therefore, all of this is key to remember from this first and only occurrence of the word "apostolos" in Matthew.

What we next need to learn about apostles is found in the second occurrence in Scripture, which is at Mark 6:30, which is also the only occurrence found in Mark. But before we look at that verse, we need to note a statement which God makes at Mark 3:13-19, which is a parallel account to what we just read above at Matthew 10:1-5, noting now what God there tells us, "[Mark 3:13] And He went up on the mountain and summoned those whom He Himself wanted, and they came to Him. [14] And He appointed twelve, so that they would be with Him and that He could send them out to preach, [15] and to have authority to cast out the demons. [16] And He appointed the twelve: Simon (to whom He gave the name Peter), [17] and James, the son of Zebedee, and John the brother of James (to them He gave the name Boanerges, which means, "Sons of Thunder"); [18] and Andrew, and Philip, and Bartholomew, and Matthew, and Thomas, and James the son of Alphaeus, and Thaddaeus, and Simon the Zealot; [19] and Judas Iscariot, who betrayed Him." We now know from Matthew 10:1-5 that the twelve at Mark 3:14 above are the apostles, with the additional information we are being given here being that "He (God's Son) appointed twelve, so that they would be with Him and that He could send them out to preach..." This is very important information for us to remember regarding those who were apostles, for we are being told here that the twelve were chosen to be with God's Son while on earth, to be trained and then to be sent out to preach!

Now that we have this information, let us look at the second occurrence of the word "apostolos" at Mark 6:30, adding verses

7 and 12 for context, "[7] And He summoned the twelve and began to send them out in pairs, and gave them authority over the unclean spirits... [12] They went out and preached that men should repent... [30] The apostles gathered together with Jesus; and they reported to Him all that they had done and taught." What needs to be observed here is that the twelve apostles are clearly in view at verse 30, who we see at verses 7 and 12 as having been sent out to preach and cast out demons, before returning to God's precious Son, Jesus Christ, to tell Him all they had done and taught. What is clear here is that the twelve apostles are only being trained at this point and have not officially begun their ministry as apostles. It is important to remember this as we proceed.

The third occurrence of the word "apostles" in Scripture is found at Luke 6:13, where we will also look at verses 12 to 16 for context, "[12] It was at this time that He went off to the mountain to pray, and He spent the whole night in prayer to God. [13] And when day came, He called His disciples to Him and chose twelve of them, whom He also named as apostles: [14] Simon, whom He also named Peter, and Andrew his brother; and James and John; and Philip and Bartholomew; [15] and Matthew and Thomas; James the son of Alphaeus, and Simon who was called the Zealot; [16] Judas the son of James, and Judas Iscariot, who became a traitor." It is clear here that this is a parallel passage to Matthew 10 and also Mark 3, with the additional information to be gathered here and kept in mind is that at verse 13 we see that God's Son had more disciples than just the twelve. In other words, the twelve, who were appointed "apostles," were taken from a larger group of disciples. What would be helpful here is knowing that the word "disciple" in God's word refers to one who was a believer and who followed God's precious Son, Jesus Christ, for the purpose of learning from Him the teachings. Therefore, those who are referred to as "disciples" are always to be seen as believers who were not only being taught the word of God, but who also adhered to it. And so it is clear from Luke 6:13 above that God's Son, while carrying out His public ministry on earth had many more disciples than just the twelve, who had been designated as apostles and who were with Him for the purpose of being trained.

Then in noting the only occurrence of the word "apostolos" at John 13:16, we see that it is not rendered as "apostles," but rather as God's Son uses it as "one... sent," as we now see, "Truly, truly, I say to you, a slave is not greater than his master, nor is one who is sent greater than the one who sent him." The reason this was brought up here is to introduce a very important truth at John 20:21, where we read, "So Jesus said to them again, "Peace be with you; as the Father has sent Me, I also send you." What is important about this is that now God's precious Son, Jesus Christ, is about to be arrested, leading to His being crucified the next morning. And so God's Son will soon be returning to Heaven again and He is turning the ministry over to the twelve to carry out, who are here in view at John 20:21. In other words, these twelve apostles, whom God's Son was earlier seen to appoint, who were with Him for three and half years that they might be trained, are now officially sent out, that they might now begin to carry out their God-given ministry focusing on preaching publicly.

What is also very important to notice and keep in mind in this regard here is that the word "apostolos" occurs 80 times in the New Testament, with only 9 occurrences in Matthew, Mark, Luke, and John, with the other 71 occurrences being AFTER they had been sent out officially by God's Son, as we see at John 20:21 above. Conversely, if one were to look at the occurrences of the word "twelve" in reference to the twelve apostles in the New Testament, one would find that there are 33 such references, with 31 in Matthew, Mark, Luke, and John, and only 2 in the rest of the New Testament after being officially sent out. What this means then is that the original twelve apostles of God's precious Son, Jesus Christ, whom He personally selected at the beginning of His ministry, were principally referred to as "the twelve" while God's Son was personally on earth, but once they had been officially sent out as apostles, as we saw at John 20:21 above, then they were officially called "apostles" from that point onwards. What this further means then, is that when one sets out to find out about an apostle, and what an apostle does, one has to principally look at the apostles beginning with Acts and the letters of the New Testament which follows. In other words, although we are introduced to apostles in the four gospel accounts of Matthew, Mark, Luke, and John, nevertheless, they are not seen as fully functioning until the start of the church age at Acts 2 and onwards, which is what will now be looking at.

b) The appointment of Matthias to bring the number to twelve apostles again just before the official start of their public ministry

By the time we reach the beginning of the book of Acts, we have the death, burial, and resurrection from the dead of God's precious Son, Jesus Christ, having taken place, with God's Son being on earth yet forty days so that His disciples might see him alive, and especially the twelve apostles, who are to lead the ministry. And what would be helpful here is to see this from Acts 1:1-5, where God tells us, "[1] The first account I composed, Theophilus, about all that Jesus began to do and teach, [2] until the day when He was taken up to heaven, after He had by the Holy Spirit given orders to the apostles whom He had chosen. [3] To these He also presented Himself alive after His suffering, by many convincing proofs, appearing to them over a period of forty days and speaking of the things concerning the kingdom of God. [4] Gathering them together, He commanded them not to leave Jerusalem, but to wait for what the Father had promised, "Which," He said, "you heard of from Me; [5] for John baptized with water, but you will be baptized with the Holy Spirit not many days from now." It is obvious here that the "apostles" in view at verse 2 are the twelve we have seen in the gospel accounts, minus Judas Iscariot, who is now dead, having committed suicide (Matthew 27:3-5). And as we see at verses 4 and 5, the apostle's ministry was not to begin until the coming of the Holy Spirit from Heaven.

But before the ministry of the apostles officially begins with the coming of The precious Holy Spirit to permanently indwell all believers on earth and to begin the church age, as we see take place at Acts 2:1-4, we have the matter of Matthias being chosen from among the disciples to replace Judas Iscariot as one of the apostles, bringing the total up to twelve again as the church age begins, noting what we read at Acts 1:23-26, "[23] So they put forward two men, Joseph called Barsabbas (who was also called Justus), and Matthias. [24] And they prayed and said, "You, Lord, who know the hearts of all men, show which one of these two You have chosen [25] to occupy this ministry and apostleship from which Judas turned aside to go to his own place." [26] And they drew lots for them, and the lot fell to Matthias; and he was added to the eleven apostles." Now that there are twelve apostles, all chosen by God's Son personally, their public ministry of preaching the gospel can now officially begin.

c) Some key truths to remember regarding the role of an apostle during the early church age

i. The apostles preached the gospel in a public ministry

If we look at Acts 2:14, we see that after the coming of The precious Holy Spirit to indwell all the believers on earth at verses 1 to 4, which event begins the church age in which we are still presently in, we have Peter, as the God-appointed leader of the twelve apostles, stand up with the other eleven apostles and begin to preach publicly to those gathered in Jerusalem on the day of Pentecost, noting what we read at Acts 2:14, "But Peter, taking his stand with the eleven, raised his voice and declared to them: "Men of Judea and all you who live in Jerusalem, let this be known to you and give heed to my words."

And what is very important to observe and remember here, which is also true in every other message preached by an apostle, which is recorded for us in Acts, is that the gospel is being preached publicly for the purpose of seeing human beings come to know God in a personal way in salvation. We must recall here that the gospel, as we have seen already earlier in the book, is concerning God's precious Son, Jesus Christ, especially focusing on His death for our sins, His burial, and His subsequent resurrection from the dead the third day. And this can be seen here in Peter's message in Jerusalem on the day of Pentecost, noting that at Acts 2:22-24, Peter is led of God to say to those listening, "[22] Men of Israel, listen to these words: Jesus the Nazarene, a man attested to you by God with miracles and wonders and signs which God performed through Him in your midst, just as you yourselves know — [23] this Man, delivered over by the predetermined plan and foreknowledge of

God, you nailed to a cross by the hands of godless men and put Him to death. [24] But God raised Him up again, putting an end to the agony of death, since it was impossible for Him to be held in its power." Let us note here that at verse 22, we have Jesus, God's Son now in human flesh being preached, with His death being mentioned at verse 23 and His resurrection from the dead being mentioned at verse 24, with His burial being understood. Then we read at verse 41 what the result was to this public preaching of the gospel by an apostle, "So then, those who had received his word were baptized; and that day there were added about three thousand souls." So it is important to see here that apostles were raised of God in the early church age to preach the gospel publicly so as to see human beings come to personally know God in salvation.

ii. The role of apostles in relation to the local church

One important truth which needs to be established here, which has a bearing on evangelists later, is the role apostles had in relation to the local church. And one good place to begin is the role of the original eleven apostles, plus Matthias later added to replace Judas Iscariot, which they had in relation to the first local church ever established by God, which was at Jerusalem. And here we can note what God tells us regarding this local church at Jerusalem during the time the twelve apostles were there, noting Acts 4:32-37, where we read, "[32] And the congregation of those who believed were of one heart and soul; and not one of them claimed that anything belonging to him was his own, but all things were common property to them. [33] And with great power the apostles were giving testimony to the resurrection of the Lord Jesus, and abundant grace was upon them all. [34] For there was not a needy person among them, for all who were owners of land or houses would sell them and bring the proceeds of the sales [35] and lay them at the apostles' feet, and they would be distributed to each as any had need. [36] Now Joseph, a Levite of Cyprian birth, who was also called Barnabas by the apostles (which translated means Son of Encouragement), [37] and who owned a tract of land, sold it and brought the money and laid it at the apostles' feet." And the truth to be noticed here is that the apostles, these being the eleven of the original twelve plus Matthias, are now still the principal and only authority in the local church at Jerusalem, with the believers there likely being mostly the result of their preaching ministry. And what is also important for us to note here is that at this point God had not yet raised elders from among the believers in the local church at Jerusalem to take over the responsibility for the believers there. What this meant then regarding the role of apostles in relation to a local church is that apostles were to remain and see the believers of a local church, which existed as a result of their gospel preaching ministry, be rooted in the faith until such time as God raised elders from among the believers to carry on the work of bringing these believers to spiritual maturity in Christ.

iii) The only two spiritual tools apostles have in order to function under God once in ministry

Another important truth to be aware of, which also relates to evangelists later on, is that at the beginning of the church age, God left apostles with only two spiritual tools to function under God once their public ministry had officially started. And here we can look at what we read at Acts 6:1-4 to see what these two tools were, "[1] Now at this time while the disciples were increasing in number, a complaint arose on the part of the Hellenistic Jews against the native Hebrews, because their widows were being overlooked in the daily serving of food. [2] So the twelve summoned the congregation of the disciples and said, "It is not desirable for us to neglect the word of God in order to serve tables. [3] Therefore, brethren, select from among you seven men of good reputation, full of the Spirit and of wisdom, whom we may put in charge of this task. [4] But we will devote ourselves to prayer and to the ministry of the word." We need to notice here that the twelve apostles were not willing to get involved in the temporal affairs of the local church, for they had been appointed by God for the spiritual welfare and growth of the believers. And what is important for our present purpose here is noting at verse 4 that they are to carry out their ministry under God with the only two tools which He left them, which is "prayer and the ministry of the word" (of God)! It is also important to keep in mind that this also became the only two tools of the elders, which God later raised for each local church on earth, and also of the evangelists.

iv. There were other apostles raised of God apart from the original twelve

Another truth which we need to be aware of regarding apostles in the early church age is that God raised other apostles apart from the original twelve, this especially being seen taking place after other local churches started being established apart from the original local church which was established at Jerusalem. One key passage to see this taking place here is noting what we read at Acts 13:1-4, "[1] Now there were at Antioch, in the church that was there, prophets and teachers: Barnabas, and Simeon who was called Niger, and Lucius of Cyrene, and Manaen who had been brought up with Herod the tetrarch, and Saul. [2] While they were ministering to the Lord and fasting, the Holy Spirit said, "Set apart for Me Barnabas and Saul for the work to which I have called them." [3] Then, when they had fasted and prayed and laid their hands on them, they sent them away. [4] So, being sent out by the Holy Spirit, they went down to Seleucia and from there they sailed to Cyprus." So now we are in a local church at Antioch in Syria, where we have five leaders of the local church gathered in prayer, three of them being identified as prophets and two as teachers, these being Barnabas and Saul (later to be known as Paul), as we will see shortly. So we see at verse 2 that God makes His will known, which is to set Barnabas and Saul apart for the work to which He is calling them to, further noting at verse 4 that it was God Who was sending them out, doing so by His Holy Spirit indwelling them in their spirit. This is why later, the apostle Paul was led to state at Galatians 1:1 in this regard, "Paul, an apostle (not sent from men nor through the agency of man, but through Jesus Christ and God the Father, who raised Him from the dead)..." This truth, namely of being sent by God, was seen to apply to the original twelve, as we have seen, and continued to be applied to every apostle subsequently raised of God in the early church age. It is also very important to note here that when God says at the end of verse 2, "the work to which I have called them...," that this referred to the call of God to apostleship for both Barnabas and Saul. In other words, all apostles would have had that call of God upon their lives, noting for instance at Matthew 10:1 and Mark 3:13 such a call in regards to the original twelve apostles.

What also needs to be remembered here is that an apostle is "one sent forth," which is what was happening to Barnabas and Saul here, which is why we then see both being referred to as "apostles" at Acts 14:4 and 14, looking at verses 1 to 14 here for context, and also for the purpose of seeing that their ministry was the same as that of the original twelve apostles, "[1] In Iconium they entered the synagogue of the Jews together, and spoke in such a manner that a large number of people believed, both of Jews and of Greeks. [2] But the Jews who disbelieved stirred up the minds of the Gentiles and embittered them against the brethren. [3] Therefore they spent a long time there speaking boldly with reliance upon the Lord, who was testifying to the word of His grace, granting that signs and wonders be done by their hands. [4] But the people of the city were divided; and some sided with the Jews, and some with the apostles. [5] And when an attempt was made by both the Gentiles and the Jews with their rulers, to mistreat and to stone them, [6] they became aware of it and fled to the cities of Lycaonia, Lystra and Derbe, and the surrounding region; [7] and there they continued to preach the gospel. [8] At Lystra a man was sitting who had no strength in his feet, lame from his mother's womb, who had never walked. [9] This man was listening to Paul as he spoke, who, when he had fixed his gaze on him and had seen that he had faith to be made well, [10] said with a loud voice, "Stand upright on your feet." And he leaped up and began to walk. [11] When the crowds saw what Paul had done, they raised their voice, saying in the Lycaonian language, "The gods have become like men and have come down to us." [12] And they began calling Barnabas, Zeus, and Paul, Hermes, because he was the chief speaker. [13] The priest of Zeus, whose temple was just outside the city, brought oxen and garlands to the gates, and wanted to offer sacrifice with the crowds. [14] But when the apostles Barnabas and Paul heard of it, they tore their robes and rushed out into the crowd, crying out..." At both verses 4 and 14, we see Barnabas and Paul being referred to as "apostles" by God, because that is what they now were, having had God's call upon their lives and now having been sent out by Him. And as was true for the original twelve apostles, so it is also true for all apostles subsequently raised of God in the various local churches, namely that they had been sent forth of God for the public preaching of the gospel, so that human beings might come to come to know God in salvation, as we see take place above for instance at verses 1 and 7.

v. Supernatural sign gifts accompanied all apostles

Another very important truth to notice and remember regarding all apostles is that God granted them supernatural sign gifts, which were for the purpose of authenticating the messengers and their message as being from God. We see this as being true first of all in regards to God's own precious Son in human flesh, Jesus Christ, while He was on earth carrying out His public ministry, noting what we read at Acts 2:22, "Men of Israel, listen to these words: Jesus the Nazarene, a man attested to you by God with miracles and wonders and signs which God performed through Him in your midst, just as you yourselves know..." The same was then true of the twelve apostles, who had been trained by God's precious Son, once they had started their public ministry, noting what we read at Acts 2:43, "Everyone kept feeling a sense of awe; and many wonders and signs were taking place through the apostles." And the same remained also true for all other apostles subsequently raised of God after the original twelve, noting what God says above at Acts 14:3 regarding both the apostles Barnabas and Paul, "Therefore they spent a long time there speaking boldly with reliance upon the Lord, who was testifying to the word of His grace, granting that signs and wonders be done by their hands." In fact, later the apostle Paul was led of God to state that spiritual sign gifts was how one would be able to recognize one who had been raised of God as an apostle, noting what we read at 2 Corinthians 12:12, "The signs of a true apostle were performed among you with all perseverance, by signs and wonders and miracles."

vi. Deacons are appointed by a local church, but elders are appointed by an apostle

Yet another truth which needs to be mentioned here which relates to apostles, and which is later to become important also in regards to the evangelists, is that after local churches became established through the preaching of the gospel by the apostles, God over time then raised elders in each local church to carry on the ministry, with these elders being appointed by the apostles. But before these elders were ever raised of God and appointed by an apostle, God did provide for the establishment of deacons in each local church, which were men chosen by the believers of each local church to assist the apostles by looking after the temporal affairs of that local church. One key passage where we see this occurring is at Acts 6:1-6, having already noted verses 1 to 4 but including them here again for context, "[1] Now at this time while the disciples were increasing in number, a complaint arose on the part of the Hellenistic Jews against the native Hebrews, because their widows were being overlooked in the daily serving of food. [2] So the twelve summoned the congregation of the disciples and said, "It is not desirable for us to neglect the word of God in order to serve tables. [3] Therefore, brethren, select from among you seven men of good reputation, full of the Spirit and of wisdom, whom we may put in charge of this task. [4] But we will devote ourselves to prayer and to the ministry of the word." [5] The statement found approval with the whole congregation; and they chose Stephen, a man full of faith and of the Holy Spirit, and Philip, Prochorus, Nicanor, Timon, Parmenas and Nicolas, a proselyte from Antioch. [6] And these they brought before the apostles; and after praying, they laid their hands on them." That the men we see being selected at verse 3 by the believers of the local church were deacons can be grasped from what God tells us at Philippians 1:1, when mentioning those in a position of authority in the local church, "Paul and Timothy, bond-servants of Christ Jesus, to all the saints in Christ Jesus who are in Philippi, including the overseers and deacons..." The overseers here were the elders, as can be grasped from comparing the list of qualifications for an overseer at 1 Timothy 3:1-8 and those for an elder at Titus 1:5-9, which are the same;

114

and also noting that at Titus 1:5 we have "elders" mentioned, with the word "overseer" being used at verse 7 when referring to the same men.

Another passage relating to deacons is found at 1 Timothy 3:8-13, where God speaks of their qualifications (with verse 11 being a reference to the deacons' wives, with deacons being in view both before and after this verse), "[8] Deacons likewise must be men of dignity, not double-tongued, or addicted to much wine or fond of sordid gain, [9] but holding to the mystery of the faith with a clear conscience. [10] These men must also first be tested; then let them serve as deacons if they are beyond reproach. [11] Women (that is, deacons' wives) must likewise be dignified, not malicious gossips, but temperate, faithful in all things. [12] Deacons must be husbands of only one wife, and good managers of their children and their own households. [13] For those who have served well as deacons obtain for themselves a high standing and great confidence in the faith that is in Christ Jesus."

And as to the truth that God used apostles in the early church to appoint the elders, whom He had raised in each local church, we are to note what God tells us at Acts 14:19-23, "[19] But Jews came from Antioch and Iconium, and having won over the crowds, they stoned Paul and dragged him out of the city, supposing him to be dead. [20] But while the disciples stood around him, he got up and entered the city. The next day he went away with Barnabas to Derbe. [21] After they had preached the gospel to that city and had made many disciples, they returned to Lystra and to Iconium and to Antioch, [22] strengthening the souls of the disciples, encouraging them to continue in the faith, and saying, "Through many tribulations we must enter the kingdom of God." [23] When they had appointed elders for them in every church, having prayed with fasting, they commended them to the Lord in whom they had believed." We have seen already from Acts 14:4 and 14 that both Paul and Barnabas were apostles, and now we clearly see that they have the responsibility before God to appoint the elders in each local church which God had started through their public ministry of preaching the gospel. It was God Who had raised these elders in each local church, who were now recognized as operating as such and therefore appointed by the apostles who were led of God to begin each of these local churches. These elders would now be carrying on the spiritual ministry of seeing the believers of that local church to now grow to spiritual maturity in Christ, having been rooted in the faith under the apostles.

At Titus 1:5, we see Titus, who was a ministry partner with the apostle Paul in the preaching of the gospel (2 Corinthians 8:23), and therefore either an apostle or an evangelist himself, being left on the island of Crete for the purpose of appointing elders in every city where local churches had been established, as we there read, "For this reason I left you in Crete, that you would set in order what remains and appoint elders in every city as I directed you..." Titus would have been with the apostle Paul on the island of Crete, also preaching the gospel there as an apostle or an evangelist like Timothy, for him to now be in a position of appointing elders, which would also be as we have seen above, where he simply would have appointed the men who were clearly being raised of God and exhibiting the qualifications which God had given for elders in a local church.

Even the local church in Jerusalem, which we saw above at Acts 4 had only the twelve apostles at the beginning, later in Acts 15, we see a fully functioning eldership there, even though there were still some of the twelve still present, noting what God tells us at Acts 15:1-4, where we read, "[1] Some men came down from Judea and began teaching the brethren (in Antioch in Syria), "Unless you are circumcised according to the custom of Moses, you cannot be saved." [2] And when Paul and Barnabas had great dissension and debate with them, the brethren determined that Paul and Barnabas and some others of them should go up to Jerusalem to the apostles and elders concerning this issue. [3] Therefore, being sent on their way by the church, they were passing through both Phoenicia and Samaria, describing in detail the conversion of the Gentiles, and were bringing great joy to all the brethren. [4] When they arrived at Jerusalem, they were received by the church and the apostles and the elders, and they reported all that God had done with them." At both verses 2 and 4 here, we have the mention of elders now having been raised of God in the local church at Jerusalem, who would have been appointed by the apostles who were led of God to begin that local church.

vii. The majority of the apostles were married men, who were allowed by God to take their believing wives along with them in their gospel ministry

Another revealing truth which needs to be mentioned in regards to the apostles of the church age, which truth also has import later for the evangelists, is that the majority of the apostles, both the twelve and those who came after, were married men who were allowed of God to take a believing wife along in their gospel ministry. Since we have seen that the word "apostle" refers to 'one sent forth,' then it was clear that these men had a ministry which took them away from home. This is clear from the book of Acts in the New Testament, where we can follow the footsteps of the twelve apostles at first, followed by the later apostles raised of God, namely the apostle Paul and Barnabas. The one revealing statement which would be of help in noting here is what God led the apostle Paul to say at 1 Corinthians 9:5, "Do we not have a right to take along a believing wife, even as the rest of the apostles and the brothers of the Lord and Cephas?" We know for sure that the apostle Paul was a man who was single to the end of his life on earth, having been given the gift of celibacy by God, as is clear from 1 Corinthians 7:6. However, as we see above, all the other apostles were married men (possibly also excluding Barnabas, for the apostle Paul says "we" at 1 Corinthians 9:5 above), who were allowed of God to take a believing wife along with them, and obviously did, as recorded here, although that fact is not recorded anywhere in Acts.

viii. Apostles only existed in the church age until God had completed giving the letters (canon) of the New Testament to His church on earth

As we bring our look at apostles to a close, there is one last very critical truth which we need to be aware of and remember, which will now also introduce us to the TRANSITION made by God to replace an apostle with an evangelist during the church age, with the truth in view here being what God tells us at Ephesians 4:7,8,11-13, where we read, "[7] But to each one of us grace was given according to the measure of Christ's gift. [8] Therefore it says, "When He ascended on high, He led captive a host of captives, and He gave gifts to men... [11] And He gave some as apostles, and some as prophets, and some as evangelists, and some as pastors and teachers, [12] for the equipping of the saints for the work of service, to the building up of the body of Christ; [13] until we all attain to the unity of the faith, and of the knowledge of the Son of God, to a mature man, to the measure of the stature which belongs to the fullness of Christ." We note here from verse 8 above that spiritual gifts were bestowed upon men in local churches on earth by God's precious Son, Jesus Christ, after His ascension back to Heaven, with God's grace being given in accordance with the measure of the gift given, as we see from verse 7. Then we see from verse 11 that the "gifts" in view here, which are men (and it is important to keep in mind that God only raises men here, noting 1 Corinthians 14:34,35 with 1 Timothy 2:11,12) given by God to local churches on earth, are apostles, prophets, evangelists, and pastor/teachers (with the word "pastor" here being a rendering of the translators, not being a Biblical word. The Biblical word here is 'shepherd,' so that the rendering should have been 'shepherd/teachers,' which is how it will be rendered in the remainder of this book).

Then the critical truth to grasp here is that apostles and prophets were only in public ministry from the start of the church on earth, starting at Acts 2:1-4, until the apostle John died in the last decade of the first century AD. In other words, apostles and prophets were only in existence in the early church until all the letters comprising the New Testament had been given to the church on earth by God. When all the letters (the canon) comprising the New Testament had been given by God, then God only raised evangelists and shepherd/teachers in the local churches from that time onward, that is, until the end of the present church age. What this means is that the apostles then are the evangelists now, while the prophets then are the shepherd/teachers now! This truth is a critical one to grasp and remember.

What also needs to be grasped here is that the men whom God had as prophets in the local churches had the sign gift of prophecy, noting 1 Corinthians 12:10, which meant that until all the letters of the New Testament had been given to the churches by God, then these men were used of God to give His word orally in each local church, until such time as that word had been permanently written down in the letters comprising the New Testament, specifically the teaching which was needful for the proper functioning of the local churches. We see such prophets in action at 1 Corinthians 14:26-33, where we read of what took place in a typical local church when the believers gathered together on The Lord's Day, "[26] What is the outcome then, brethren? When you assemble, each one has a psalm, has a teaching, has a revelation, has a tongue, has an interpretation. Let all things be done for edification. [27] If anyone speaks in a tongue, it should be by two or at the most three, and each in turn, and one must interpret; [28] but if there is no interpreter, he must keep silent in the church; and let him speak to himself and to God. [29] Let two or three prophets speak, and let the others pass judgment. [30] But if a revelation is made to another who is seated, the first one must keep silent. [31] For you can all prophesy one by one, so that all may learn and all may be exhorted; [32] and the spirits of prophets are subject to prophets; [33] for God is not a God of confusion but of peace, as in all the churches of the saints." As we see at verse 30, the mention of a "revelation" would be what the supernatural sign gift of prophecy enabled these prophets to do, which was to make known God's will as expressed in His word until such time as each of the letters comprising the New Testament had been given to the churches by God. Once all the letters of the New Testament had been given by God, then there was no longer any need for the gift of prophecy, nor of prophets to exercise it. And once God raised shepherd/teachers to replace them, then there was no more need for the revelations through the prophets with the sign gift of prophecy since all the truth God wanted to give the churches on earth was now contained in the letters of the New Testament, so that shepherd/teachers only needed to teach God's word to the people gathered each Lord's Day as the truth of the written word was illumined to them by The Holy Spirit indwelling them.

119

And the same can also be said about the sign gifts which accompanied the apostles, which we have already noted was exercised by all the apostles. These sign gifts also all ceased with the passing of the apostles from the scene on earth, so that no true evangelist raised of God has ever been known to have any of the sign gifts. Actually, the reverse is true now, those who claim to have them can be seen as simply not being of God, same as the sign gifts in the early church actually identified one as being a true apostle. Therefore, it is not surprising to read what the apostle John was led of God to write to the local church at Ephesus at Revelation 2:2, "I know your deeds and your toil and perseverance, and that you cannot tolerate evil men, and you put to the test those who call themselves apostles, and they are not, and you found them to be false..." One of the tests would have been whether they had supernatural ability from God to do signs, wonders, and miracles, for God had by that point in time stopped giving apostles and prophets to the local churches, these being now replaced by evangelists and shepherd/teachers.

One very important passage we can look at here where God shows that the apostles and prophets were only for the early church is to note what He says to us at Ephesians 2:17-20, where we read, "[17] And He came and preached peace to you who were far away, and peace to those who were near; [18] for through Him we both have our access in one Spirit to the Father. [19] So then you are no longer strangers and aliens, but you are fellow citizens with the saints, and are of God's household, [20] having been built on the foundation of the apostles and prophets, Christ Jesus Himself being the corner stone..." The important truth being shared here by God is that God's household, made up of the believers of the present church age, has "been built on the foundation of the apostles and prophets," with God's precious Son, Jesus Christ, being the corner stone of that foundation. Once that foundation had been laid by means of the apostles and prophets, which work was completed in the first century AD with all the letters of the New Testament having been given by God to His church on earth by then, God had no more need of apostles and prophets, from then on raising only evangelists and shepherd/teachers.

And if we now come back to Ephesians 2:12 and 13 above, we were told there by God that the gifted men of verse 11 had been raised of God and given to each local church, namely the apostles and prophets at first, and the evangelists and shepherd/teachers later on, had a God-given purpose to fulfill. We see that purpose as being "for the equipping of the saints for the work of service, to the building up of the body of Christ; until we all attain to the unity of the faith, and of the knowledge of the Son of God, to a mature man, to the measure of the stature which belongs to the fullness of Christ." In other words, the apostles and prophets at first, and then the evangelists and shepherd/teachers afterwards, had the God-given ministry of equipping the believers comprising the local churches so that they would fulfill their spiritual service to God as His children yet on earth, so that the church as a whole might not only attain to the unity of the faith given by God, but that all together might grow to the spiritual maturity which is full conformity to God's own and precious Son, Jesus Christ.

What also needs to be grasped here is that when God mentions "to the building up of the body of Christ" at verse 12, He is indicating that the apostle then, as the evangelist now, would be sent out from a local church by God for the public preaching of the gospel for the building up of the body numerically, in terms of seeing unbelievers be saved through the preaching of the word of God, and so as to see them added to the church! Similarly, the prophets then, as shepherd/teachers now, would be building up the body of Christ through the teaching of the word, so as to see these believers reach full spiritual maturity in Christ. Therefore, it is clear that God knew exactly what He was doing, both before the close of the canon of the New Testament with the apostles and prophets, and after all the letters of the New Testament had been given, with the evangelists and shepherd/teachers He was now raising.

And now that we have a better grasp of what evangelists are and do, having principally seen this from the apostles who preceded them, we can now go on to look at some key truths relating specifically to an evangelist.

THE ROLE OF THE APOSTLES AND PROPHETS IN THE EARLY CHURCH, AND OF THE EVANGELISTS AND SHEPHERD/TEACHERS IN THE LATER CHURCH, IN RELATION TO THE ELDERS AND THE TEACHING FUNCTION OF THE LOCAL CHURCH

What would be helpful here is to see the establishment and functioning of a local church as intended by God from the start of the church age at Acts 2:1-4 until that church ends with the removal of all believers from the earth at the first stage of the second coming of God's precious Son, Jesus Christ, from Heaven to earth. And so, we will look at this chapter while keeping two divisions of the present church age in view, in one looking at the early church under apostles and prophets, from around 30 to 100 AD, which is about the date by which all the letters of the New Testament had been given to man by God. Then we will look at the later church under evangelists and shepherd/teachers, which is from 100 AD to the end of the present church age. In looking at these two divisions, we will also see the relation between an apostle at first, and an evangelist later, in relation to the elders and the teaching function in the local church. And let us remember that the only ministers God ever has in a local church are as we see at Ephesians 4:11, which are apostles and prophets before the giving of the letters of the New Testament to the church by God, and then evangelists and shepherd/teachers after these letters have all been given.

When we see the church begin at Jerusalem at Acts 2:1-4, with the coming of The Holy Spirit from Heaven to permanently indwell believers on earth, we have the twelve apostles, who had been trained by God's own Son while on earth, now officially begin their public ministry of preaching the gospel. And as the gospel is preached, some believe and become part of the local church at Jerusalem. At this point, we have only the apostles in leadership. Then at Acts 6:1 to 6, we see men being appointed by the believers of the local church at Jerusalem, which we later learn are deacons, with their function being to assist the apostles, in terms of looking after the temporal affairs of the local church, while the apostles look after the spiritual affairs of the local church, by means of prayer and the ministry of the word. And that ministry of the word in relation to the believers of the local church is to teach them the word of God, so as to see them rooted and established in the faith. But what needs to be realized here is that at this point, believers only have the Old Testament available to them in written form, with the twelve apostles having knowledge of what God's precious Son, Jesus Christ, taught them during the three and a half years they walked with Him, being trained by Him to carry on the ministry on earth after He had returned to Heaven again at the ascension. What God's Son taught the twelve apostles while on earth now makes up the germ seeds for what will later form the letters of the New Testament And so, until the letters of the New Testament are given by God, written down, and circulated among the local churches, that and the Old Testament, are all the believers have to go by of the word of God.

If we jump over to Acts 13:1 for a moment, we see another local church having begun at Antioch in Syria, being here told that, "Now there were at Antioch, in the church that was there, prophets and teachers: Barnabas, and Simeon who was called Niger, and Lucius of Cyrene, and Manaen who had been brought up with Herod the tetrarch, and Saul." We have already looked at this verse in the previous chapter and seen that Barnabas and Saul (later to be referred to as Paul) were the two teachers in view here, while the other three men were the prophets. And we have also already seen that Barnabas and Paul are here being sent out by God, which sending makes them now apostles, which means they are now preachers of the gospel in public ministry. Barnabas and Paul then go to various cities where disciples are made, in that people come to a personal relationship with God in believing the gospel. The believers in each of these cities then make up the local church there. Then at Acts 14:23, which we have already also looked at, we see Paul and Barnabas, as apostles, appointing elders in each of the local churches which had been established under their ministry, before they return to the local church at Antioch from which they had gone from.

Now in returning to that local church in Antioch, we have the three men already there in leadership as prophets. They remain there and teach the believers when gathered, with Paul and Barnabas also teaching the believers when gathered, because we have mentioned before that they were teachers, which teaching function they also would have exercised in each of the local churches which God had just established under their ministry, rooting and establishing the believers in each local church until such time as God raised elders. So both apostles and prophets exercised the teaching function in the church gathered, although the apostles were only exercising the teaching function before being sent out by God, but afterwards also being preachers of the gospel, which was primarily to the unsaved.

Now as to the matter of elders, we are to note first of all that to be an elder is to hold an office in a local church, while to be an apostle, prophet, evangelist, or shepherd/teacher is to be a gift given by God to the church universal. An apostle at first, as is true of an evangelist now, is not a man gifted by God with the gift of evangelism, as some may think, but rather is himself a gift in his person to the church existing on earth, which is comprised of all believers yet on earth. That an elder holds an office is seen from what God says at 1 Timothy 3:1, where we read, "It is a trustworthy statement: if any man aspires to the office of overseer, it is a fine work he desires to do."

As to the evangelist being a gift from God to His church on earth, we have already noted this from Ephesians 4:7,8,11. Elders are always raised of God from among the believers of a local church, being then recognized as such by the apostle at first, later by the evangelist, as the one having begun that local church through the public preaching of the gospel. One is appointed to the office of elder only after being raised of God. In other words, God is The One Who raises elders, as is clear from what we read at Acts 20:28, where God says to the elders at Ephesus through the apostle Paul, "Be on guard for yourselves and for all the flock, among which the Holy Spirit has made you overseers, to shepherd the church of God which He purchased with His own blood." It is never an apostle or an evangelist who chooses an elder. Rather, they only appoint the men that God has raised, with their being able to identify them through their functioning as such, noting the qualifications they would have based on what God gave at 1 Timothy 3:1-7 and Titus 1:5-9.

And as to the relation between these four gifted men given by God to the church in relation to the elders and the teaching function of the local church, we are to see that before they are gifted by God, which is when their ministry starts, the apostles at first, and then the evangelists, are men holding the office of elders and exercising the teaching function in the local church. In order to see this here, we can now return to the church at Jerusalem, which was the first local church established by God on earth after the church age started at Acts 2. Where we left off above, we had the twelve apostles ministering in that local church, teaching the believers when gathered. Over time, these apostles did the same in this church at Jerusalem as we saw Paul and Barnabas do in the churches they established over the known world, which was to also appoint elders there, from among the believers in that local church. That is why at Acts 15:1-6, which we have already looked at, we see elders now functioning in that church along with the twelve apostles.

One important truth which we need to be aware of is that although the twelve apostles of God's precious Son, Jesus Christ, were the original leaders of the local church at Jerusalem, which had begun through their preaching of the gospel in Jerusalem, nevertheless, they were regarded by God as elders and apostles, even though only recognized as apostles by men. Later, as the believers of that local church at Jerusalem grew spiritually under the teaching ministry of the apostles to establish them in the faith, God raised up elders from among them to carry on the ministry once the apostles were no longer there. That is why we see at Acts 1:20, where God says in regards to finding a replacement for Judas Iscariot, speaking through the apostle Peter says to us what we there read, looking at verses 16,17,20 to 26 for context, "[16] "Brethren, the Scripture had to be fulfilled, which the Holy Spirit foretold by the mouth of David concerning Judas, who became a guide to those who arrested Jesus. [17] For he was counted among us and received his share in this ministry...[20] For it is written in the book of Psalms, 'Let his homestead be made desolate, and let no one dwell in it'; and, 'Let another man take his office.' [21] Therefore it is necessary that of the men who have accompanied us all the time that the Lord Jesus went in and out among us — [22] beginning with the baptism of John until the day that He was taken up from us — one of these must become a witness with us of His resurrection." [23] So they put forward two men, Joseph called Barsabbas (who was also called Justus), and Matthias. [24] And they prayed and said, "You, Lord, who know the hearts of all men, show which one of these two You have chosen [25] to occupy this ministry and apostleship from which Judas turned aside to go to his own place." [26] And they drew lots for them, and the lot fell to Matthias; and he was added to the eleven apostles." We need to note at verse 20 that the word "office" here is the same Greek word as at 1 Timothy 3:1 and literally refers to the same 'office of overseer' that was there in view, which means that Judas Iscariot had this office of an elder as one of the twelve apostles, and which Matthias, as his replacement among the twelve, was now to have, as is clear from verse 25. And so, it was because the apostles were also elders that the apostle Peter refers himself as an elder at 1 Peter 5:1, when addressing believers, "Therefore, I exhort the elders among you, as your fellow elder..." Similarly for the apostle John at 2 John 1:1 and 3 John 1:1. Although the word "elder" has an age component inherent in the word throughout Scripture, and even though the apostle John is no doubt an aged man when led of God to write this, nevertheless, he was not just an apostle, but also an elder in the church.

And coming back full circle to the local church at Antioch in Syria, Paul and Barnabas were elders in that local church before being sent out by God as apostles, where they had been exercising the teaching function, along with the other three elders who were prophets. What this means is that the men to be elders in a local church are teachers until such time as raised of God as elders and then appointed as such by the apostle responsible for establishing that local church. When appointed as an elder, one holds the office of elder, being either gifted by God as an apostle or a prophet. If an elder is gifted as an apostle, then God will send out that elder at some point, which means one has now a call of God and is now sent out by God as an apostle, still holding the office of elder. After all the letters of the New Testament had been given by 100 AD, then elders of local churches throughout the world were either being gifted by God as evangelists or shepherd/teachers, and no longer as apostles and prophets.

Now that we know that the apostles of the early church were replaced by the evangelists, which is to be the case right up to the end of the present church age, we can now quickly summarize what still applies and what does not, relating to what an apostle did then and what an evangelist does now. Evangelist are still sent out by God to preach the gospel in public ministry, having the same two tools available to apostles, that being prayer and the ministry of the word of God. Whereas supernatural sign gifts accompanied the ministry of apostles, yet now for evangelists, all such sign gifts have ceased. Evangelists are also men, who if married are also allowed to take a believing wife along in the public preaching of the gospel.

KEY TRUTHS RELATING TO AN EVANGELIST

What we would like to do in this chapter is to look at a number of key truths relating to an evangelist, which have been applicable in the church since God started raising evangelists shortly after He began the church on earth. These key truths will now be examined under the following headings:

1) Evangelists are men raised of God with the main task of preaching the gospel

We have already noted that the word "apostle" referred to 'one sent forth,' that being from God and not men. Now we are to see that the word "evangelist" refers to 'a bringer of good news.' And in this regard, we need to note a very key passage, which is at Romans 10:13-15, where God is talking now specifically about evangelists, there saying to us,"[13] for "Whoever will call on the name of the Lord will be saved." [14] How then will they call on Him in whom they have not believed? How will they believe in Him whom they have not heard? And how will they hear without a preacher? [15] How will they preach unless they are sent? Just as it is written, "How beautiful are the feet of those who bring good news of good things!" " At the end of verse 14 here, God asks a very pertinent question, "how will they hear without a preacher?," then going on at the beginning of verse 15 to ask another very important question, which is, "How will they preach unless they are sent?" And here we note that one cannot preach unless one is sent, because only in the sending does God provide the spiritual enablement to preach the gospel in public ministry! Does this not sound familiar, in terms of being exactly what we have seen in regards to an apostle? What this means then is that one's ministry as an evangelist begins the same way as with an apostle, only when one is sent from God, and not from men. Only then is one an evangelist, a preacher of good news, that is, a preacher of the gospel, which is a public ministry, as was the case with the apostle. And what is also important to note here is that a prophet before, as is also the case with the shepherd/teacher now, are never referred to as 'preachers of the gospel.' Such terminology was solely reserved for the apostles at first, and now for the evangelists!

Therefore, we need to emphasize again that the main task for which an evangelist has been raised of God is to preach the gospel in public ministry, which was also the case with the apostles raised of God. And here we can note what the apostle Paul was led of God to say at 1 Corinthians 1:17 in part and then at 1 Corinthians 9:16,17, which would be true also of every evangelist ever raised of God, "For Christ did not send me to baptize, but to preach the gospel... For if I preach the gospel, I have nothing to boast of, for I am under compulsion; for woe is me if I do not preach the gospel. For if I do this voluntarily, I have a reward; but if against my will, I have a stewardship entrusted to me." When the apostle Paul says here, "I have a stewardship entrusted to me," he is referring to the day we have seen from Acts 13:1-4 when he and Barnabas were approved of God to be entrusted with the gospel and then sent out by God, which the apostle Paul further makes reference to at 1 Thessalonians 2:4, "but just as we have been approved by God to be entrusted with the gospel, so we speak, not as pleasing men, but God who examines our hearts." And since evangelists have now replaced apostles in the church on earth, then this is also true of all evangelists, namely that all such men have been approved by God to be entrusted with the gospel, when first called of God for such ministry and then sent out by God.

2) The second task of an evangelist is to teach

Then we are to be aware that the next task of an evangelist, after the task of preaching the gospel, is to teach, both before and after being raised of God as an evangelist. As we have seen in the previous chapter, evangelists are raised of God from men who are functioning as elders in the church, whether recognized as such or not. And as an elder one would be exercising the teaching function relating to the believers of a local church, this being clear from the fact that one of the qualifications of an elder is that one be able to teach spiritual truth, as we see at 1 Timothy 3:2 and Titus 1:9.

What is important to grasp here is that an elder never knows beforehand that one is going to be raised of God as an evangelist, although what should be evident from one's life is that one already has a heart desire to see people come to know

God in a personal relationship, with that heart desire having been placed there by God as preparation for the work He has His servant to do. In other words, God will have started to prepare one to be an evangelist before one is called of Him as such, same as the twelve apostles of God's precious Son, Jesus Christ, were trained of Him for three and half years before they were officially sent out by Him to begin their ministry as apostles. And so the same will be true in regards to elders in the church, or men in the church who should be elders, and are even functioning as elders, but for one reason or another, are never appointed as elders (keeping in mind that in these last days very few in the church are even aware of, or even practicing, the truths being shared in this book). In other words, such men will have a heart for evangelism and may even be found teaching others about evangelism in the local church where they attend, or even showing others in practice how to evangelize.

After one has been raised of God as an evangelist and sent out by God, then the teaching function is primarily, at first at least, to establish in the faith those have who come to know God through their ministry of preaching the gospel. As these believers are established, then the evangelist's teaching task is to teach them about the gospel, and how to reach others with the gospel, so as to see others come to know God in salvation, from among the circle of family, friends, and co-workers of each of these believers. An important verse we can again note in this regard is what God says at Ephesians 4:12, looking here at verse 11 to 13 for context, "[11] And He gave some as apostles, and some as prophets, and some as evangelists, and some as pastors (should be shepherds) and teachers, [12] for the equipping of the saints for the work of service, to the building up of the body of Christ; [13] until we all attain to the unity of the faith, and of the knowledge of the Son of God, to a mature man, to the measure of the stature which belongs to the fullness of Christ." When God says at verse 12 here, "for the equipping of the saints for the work of service," God has in view the evangelists teaching the believers under their care in their ministry to be vessels in God's Hands to be used of Him in sharing the gospel in their immediate circle of family, friends, and acquaintances, so that by God's grace and power some might come to know

God, thereby increasing the number of believers as the church in that locality numerically. In other words, the evangelist teaches the believers to share their faith when scattered as a local church, while the shepherd/teacher teaches the believers of that local church when gathered as a local church, so that as the body of Christ locally, they might all grow together in the unity of the faith and to spiritual maturity in Christ.

And that an evangelist is also a teacher in the church should not surprise us, since the apostles who preceded the evangelists were themselves teachers in the church, noting what the apostle Paul was led of God to say at 1 Timothy 2:7, "For this I was appointed a preacher and an apostle (I am telling the truth, I am not lying) as a teacher of the Gentiles in faith and truth," and also at 2 Timothy 1:11, "for which I was appointed a preacher and an apostle and a teacher." And of course the same is true of all evangelists now, as is clear from what the apostle Paul says to Timothy, who was an evangelist, at 2 Timothy 4:2 to 4, noting verses 1 to 5 for context, "[1] I solemnly charge you in the presence of God and of Christ Jesus, who is to judge the living and the dead, and by His appearing and His kingdom: [2] preach the word; be ready in season and out of season; reprove, rebuke, exhort, with great patience and instruction. [3] For the time will come when they will not endure sound doctrine; but wanting to have their ears tickled, they will accumulate for themselves teachers in accordance to their own desires, [4] and will turn away their ears from the truth and will turn aside to myths. [5] But you, be sober in all things, endure hardship, do the work of an evangelist, fulfill your ministry." Let us note here that after emphasizing the priority of Timothy's ministry as an evangelist as being to preach the gospel, at verse 2, the apostle Paul then goes on in the rest of verse 2 to verse 4 to emphasize his next task, which was to teach! The reference to "reprove, rebuke, exhort, with great patience and instruction" had to do with teaching, with believers being in view here. We will have more to say about Timothy as an evangelist in the next chapter.

3) Evangelists are to baptize those who come to faith until such time as God raises elders who are shepherd/teachers

When an evangelist is in his field of service and a number of people are brought to faith in God in salvation, then it would be necessary for the evangelist to baptize these believers by water immersion, since water baptism is always meant to be as soon as possible after the moment of one's salvation, noting Acts 2:41 and Acts 10:47,48. Once God raises elders from among these believers, then the task of baptizing new believers by water immersion would fall to these elders, who would be shepherd/teachers.

4) Evangelists are to appoint elders

If an evangelist is on his field of service and God has not yet raised elders from among the believers saved under one's ministry, then one has the responsibility under God to keep teaching the believers who have come to faith in God through one's ministry. The teaching involved here would be the truths we have just looked at from Ephesians 4:12 and 13, namely the truths of God's word required to establish these believers in the faith, and also the truths relating to be able to share one's faith so as to reproduce spiritually. Only when God raises elders from among the believers of one's ministry, and then directs the evangelist to appoint them, is an evangelist freed by God from leaving that field of service.

What should also be mentioned here is that once a local church has been established with elders, then future elders, to replace the one's who die, or to add to the number due to an increasing number of believers, would be appointed by the existing elders, who would have the responsibility under God to appoint the men whom God is raising as elders from among the believers in that local church. Since God has given the qualifications for what to look for, as already noted from 1 Timothy 3:2-7 and Titus 1:6-9, then the existing elders only need to wait for the call of God to come to the person being raised of God, which call will also be made known by God to the existing elders. In other words, when God's call comes for one to become an elder, or even to become an evangelist to be sent out, that call will also be communicated to the existing eldership of the local church, so that they will be able to lay hands on them to indicate that they agree with the call on that person's life as being of God and not coming from the person himself. The laying of hands would also mean that the elders fully support the ministry, not only in terms of prayer, but also in terms of financial support. God gives us the pattern for what has just been said in what He says to us at Acts 13:1-4, which we have already looked at. There we saw that it was God's call to Barnabas and Saul (Paul), when God's time came for them to be sent out as apostles, but the principle is the same for God's call to an evangelist, and also for an elder, who is to remain as a shepherd/teacher, or sent out by God as an evangelist.

5) Evangelists are always in need of prayer support

What is very important to grasp here is that since the main task of an evangelist is to preach the gospel so that human beings might come to know God in a personal relationship, then it can be expected that these are the men the devil will do his utmost to attempt to prevent from carrying out their ministry! And in order to see this, we would be helped in noting what the apostle Paul says to Timothy, who was an evangelist, at 2 Timothy 4:5, where we read, "But you, be sober in all things, endure hardship, do the work of an evangelist, fulfill your ministry." And the words we want to focus on here is when the apostle Paul says to Timothy, "endure hardship," which will not have much meaning for us until we realize that the term "endure hardship" is one word in the Greek, which literally means 'to suffer evil.' In other words, it is evil at the hands of the devil that an evangelist is constantly being confronted with.

The apostle Paul also expresses a similar truth to Timothy when he says to him at 2 Timothy 2:3, "Suffer hardship with me, as a good soldier of Christ Jesus." The term "suffer hardship" here is not the same Greek word as at 2 Timothy 4:5, but the thought is very similar, for it means 'to bear evil treatment along with.' The reality is that Satan, the devil, always works with a set purpose, which is to lead a believer into sin, and especially the leaders, and when that fails, to lead one into error, with our needing to see here that both purposes in the present case being to prevent the evangelist from carrying out one's ministry in a God honoring and effective manner. That is why the apostle Paul cautions Timothy at 1 Timothy 4:16, "Pay close attention to yourself (in terms of watching out for the temptations which are sure to come) and to your teaching (in terms of watching so as not to be led into error); persevere in these things, for as you do this you will ensure salvation both for yourself and for those who hear you." So the evangelist not only needs to watch out for these schemes of the devil himself, but believers who support the ministry can also be in prayer for the evangelist about these matters.

It is no wonder then that God says to all believers, which would be applicable to evangelists in particular, what we read at Ephesians 6:11,12, "[11] Put on the full armor of God, so that you will be able to stand firm against the schemes of the devil. [12] For our struggle is not against flesh and blood, but against the rulers, against the powers, against the world forces of this darkness, against the spiritual forces of wickedness in the heavenly places." The devil knows that if he can stop an evangelist's ministry through leading the evangelist into sin, or at least detract him through error, then he will be doing harm to God's work on earth, having temporarily at least disabled those whom God has appointed to lead the charge. And that is why prayer for evangelists by God's people is so important.

The word "schemes" in the mention of "the schemes of the devil" above, means 'to employ craft, deceit,' which is why God warns believers at 2 Corinthians 11:13-15 about the devil and his human workers he has on earth, who do not come to any believers, including evangelists, as they really are, but they use deceit to do their evil work, noting what we there read, "[13] For such men are false apostles, deceitful workers, disguising themselves as apostles of Christ. [14] No wonder, for even Satan disguises himself as an angel of light. [15] Therefore it is not surprising if his servants also disguise themselves as servants of righteousness, whose end will be according to their deeds."

And this brings up another very important mention of the word 'schemes' in relation to the devil, and where all believers need to be aware of, and especially evangelists, which is noting what God tells us at 2 Corinthians 2:11, where we read, "so that no advantage would be taken of us by Satan, for we are not ignorant of his schemes." The word "schemes" here refers 'to thought, to mental perception.' In other words, what we are being told here is that the devil uses thoughts to attempt to lead the believer, including the evangelist, from the path of God's will for one's life. One key verse where we see the devil having done this is at 2 Corinthians 11:3, where God tells us, "But I am afraid that, as the serpent deceived Eve by his craftiness, your minds will be led astray from the simplicity and purity of devotion to Christ." Please note that it is the minds of believers that the devil is here seen to want to lead believers astray by. All we have said here is especially applicable to the evangelist, who the devil knows is at the forefront of the battle against these evil forces and schemes.

I can personally testify that apart from God's grace and protection, this evangelist's ministry could not go on, for the devil continually attempts to stop it and detract it in some ways, and when that fails, even attempting to have this evangelist killed. In my second book, titled "Finding Comfort And Encouragement In The Promises Of God In The Last Days," I relate a number of occurrences where apart from God's intervention, I would have been killed. Therefore, the first thing an evangelist is in need of from other believers is prayer support, for protection from the evil one and all those he would use as his instruments, both other fallen angels, who are demons, or unbelievers here on earth. We should not be surprised to hear the apostle Paul ask believers in his day for such prayer support, noting what God records for us at 2 Thessalonians 3:1,2, "[1] Finally, brethren, pray for us that the word of the Lord will spread rapidly and be glorified, just as it did also with you; [2] and that we will be rescued from perverse and evil men; for not all have faith." That is why any evangelist now in ministry will do likewise, for the spiritual battle against the forces of evil is real, and the suffering in that battle is real also. It is no wonder that the apostle Paul used the term, "as a good soldier of Jesus Christ," at 2 Timothy 2:3, for the battle is against our enemy, the devil, and it involves the eternal destiny of human beings. The devil wants to prevent people from coming to know God, while the evangelist is simply God's vessel at the forefront of the battle, where the gospel is being shared so that one might come to know God in salvation.

6) Evangelists are more often than not in need of financial support

God makes a very revealing statement at 1 Corinthians 9:14 through the apostle Paul, which is not just applicable to apostles, but also to evangelists, when He says, "So also the Lord directed those who proclaim the gospel to get their living from the gospel." This statement here, "to get their living from the gospel," means a number of things. First of all, it means that apostles at first, and evangelists now, as those whom God sends out to preach the gospel, are to remain at the task of preaching the gospel, and while doing so, they will find supply to meet their needs in daily living. In other words, an evangelist, when called of God and sent out as an evangelist, is now employed fulltime by God in the task of preaching the gospel. Those who are evangelists are not to stop doing this in order to go work for someone else in order to earn one's living. I can personally testify to this. When called of God as an evangelist, I had the financial means to support my God-given ministry out of my own funds. However, after the financial meltdown of September 2008 and following, those funds quickly dwindled, and as a result, by October of 2013, I was totally out of funds and had to rely totally on God to provide for my support. The only thing I have been able to figure out, as to why God allowed His servant to lose a lot of his available funds, was that up to that point in my gospel ministry finances were the only area of my life where I did not have to depend on God for. And I believe God wants His servants to be fully dependent on Him in every area of their lives!

Another important truth to be grasped from God's statement at 1 Corinthians 9:14, when He says to those whom He sends out to preach the gospel, "to get their living from the gospel," is that God does not mean by this that one is to obtain funds from unbelievers, to whom the gospel is being preached. Rather, what God intends here is for those who have benefited from having the gospel preached to them, and as a result now find themselves the children of God on earth, that these are the ones who are to ensure that the evangelists they know obtain their living from their gospel ministry. In other words, it is believers, both corporately as a church, and individually, who are to financially support the ministry of evangelists. This is first applicable to those directly under the ministry of an evangelist, noting for instance what God writes to believers at Galatians 6:6, as what applied to not only the support of evangelists, but also of those who were shepherd/teachers, "The one who is taught the word is to share all good things with the one who teaches him." That is why God further says to believers through the apostle Paul at 1 Corinthians 9:11, "If we sowed spiritual things in you, is it too much if we reap material things from you?"

What is required here is for believers on earth to be walking with God, in terms of no known unconfessed sins in one's life in order to be living by God's righteousness, so that one may be available to God, in terms of carrying out His will on earth, which would include financially supporting an evangelist as God directs. Shepherd/teachers, who remain at the local church and minister there each Lord's day, are being supported by the weekly offering from the gathered believers. And this is how it should be, for this is what God directed (1 Corinthians 16:2). However, the evangelists may not be in a position to have a weekly offering taken, with God knowing who these would be, no doubt wanting believers who are available to Him to supply the need.

Where an evangelist has preached the gospel and a number of persons have become believers under one's ministry, then there would be in such cases some measure of financial support from these believers, as one instructs them in the ministry of giving. The apostle Paul's statement at 1 Corinthians 4:11 paints an unfortunate picture of the reality for many of God's servants, "To this present hour we are both hungry and thirsty, and are poorly clothed, and are roughly treated, and are homeless..." May God's people realize that God's way of meeting needs, whether for the salvation of someone, or the financial support of others, is through His available children on earth. May we all be sensitive to God's leading in these vital areas in these last days of the church age!

LOOKING AT THE TWO MEN REFERRED TO BY GOD AS BEING EVANGELISTS IN GOD'S WORD

What would be helpful to do in this chapter is to note the two men who are identified by God by name as being evangelists in His word, that being Philip at Acts 21:8 and also Timothy, at 2 Timothy 4:5. Let us see what God can further teach us about evangelists from looking at the ministry of these two men.

1) Philip, the evangelist

As mentioned above, Philip is referred to by God in His word as being an evangelist, noting what we read at Acts 21:8, "On the next day we left and came to Caesarea, and entering the house of Philip the evangelist, who was one of the seven, we stayed with him." Here we note that Philip is also being identified as being "one of the seven," which is an obvious reference to the seven men we see being chosen by the believers for the temporal affairs of the local church at Jerusalem at Acts 6:5, noting verses 1 to 6 here for context, "[1] Now at this time while the disciples were increasing in number, a complaint arose on the part of the Hellenistic Jews against the native Hebrews, because their widows were being overlooked in the daily serving of food. [2] So the twelve summoned the congregation of the disciples and said, "It is not desirable for us to neglect the word of God in order to serve tables. [3] Therefore, brethren, select from among you seven men of good reputation, full of the Spirit and of wisdom, whom we may put in charge of this task. [4] But we will devote ourselves to prayer and to the ministry of the word." [5] The statement found approval with the whole congregation; and they chose Stephen, a man full of faith and of the Holy Spirit, and Philip, Prochorus, Nicanor, Timon, Parmenas and Nicolas, a proselyte from Antioch. [6] And these they brought before the apostles; and after praying, they laid their hands on them." The men mentioned at verse 5 are the seven, whom we also identified as being the earliest deacons in the church.

The next time we encounter this same Philip in God's word is at Acts 8:4, which we are to note is immediately after the local church at Jerusalem is scattered, except the twelve apostles, due to a persecution brought on by Saul, who was later to become a believer with the name of Paul. And here it would be beneficial for us to look at what God tells us at Acts 8:1-7,13 "[1] Saul was in hearty agreement with putting him to death (that is, Stephen, the first church martyr). And on that day a great persecution began against the church in Jerusalem, and they were all scattered throughout the regions of Judea and Samaria, except the apostles. [2] Some devout men buried Stephen, and made loud lamentation over him. [3] But Saul began ravaging the church, entering house after house, and dragging off men and women, he would put them in prison. [4] Therefore, those who had been scattered went about preaching the word. [5] Philip went down to the city of Samaria and began proclaiming Christ to them. [6] The crowds with one accord were giving attention to what was said by Philip, as they heard and saw the signs which he was performing. [7] For in the case of many who had unclean spirits, they were coming out of them shouting with a loud voice; and many who had been paralyzed and lame were healed... [13] Even Simon himself believed; and after being baptized, he continued on with Philip, and as he observed signs and great miracles taking place, he was constantly amazed." Now that we have gained a lot of information from our having extensively discussed apostles in God's word, we can here clearly identify Philip as now fulfilling the ministry of an apostle, since we see from verses 4 to 7 and also from verse 13 that Philip was not only preaching the gospel publicly, but that his gospel ministry was also accompanied by supernatural gift signs, which accompanied one who had been called by God as an apostle, noting again for instance what God says at 2 Corinthians 12:12 regarding an apostle.

The next time we encounter Philip, it is at Acts 8:26, where God now uses Philip to bring the gospel to a man who was searching for God, noting what God tells us at Acts 26-40 of this encounter, "[26] But an angel of the Lord spoke to Philip saying, "Get up and go south to the road that descends from Jerusalem to Gaza." (This is a desert road.) [27] So he got up and went; and there was an Ethiopian eunuch, a court official of Candace, queen of the Ethiopians, who was in charge of all her treasure; and he had come to Jerusalem to worship, [28] and he was returning and sitting in his chariot, and was reading the prophet

Isaiah. [29] Then the Spirit said to Philip, "Go up and join this chariot." [30] Philip ran up and heard him reading Isaiah the prophet, and said, "Do you understand what you are reading?" [31] And he said, "Well, how could I, unless someone guides me?" And he invited Philip to come up and sit with him. [32] Now the passage of Scripture which he was reading was this: "He was led as a sheep to slaughter; and as a lamb before its shearer is silent, so He does not open His mouth. [33] In humiliation His judgment was taken away; who will relate His generation? For His life is removed from the earth." [34] The eunuch answered Philip and said, "Please tell me, of whom does the prophet say this? Of himself or of someone else?" [35] Then Philip opened his mouth, and beginning from this Scripture he preached Jesus to him. [36] As they went along the road they came to some water; and the eunuch said, "Look! Water! What prevents me from being baptized?" [38] And he ordered the chariot to stop; and they both went down into the water, Philip as well as the eunuch, and he baptized him. [39] When they came up out of the water, the Spirit of the Lord snatched Philip away; and the eunuch no longer saw him, but went on his way rejoicing. [40] But Philip found himself at Azotus, and as he passed through he kept preaching the gospel to all the cities until he came to Caesarea."

We know that this court official was seeking for God since he had come all the way from Ethiopia to Jerusalem to offer worship to God, Whom at this point he did not yet personally know. But his hour had come on God's timetable for him to become a child of God in salvation, so God sends Philip to join with his chariot, where we see in the above account that the man was reading Isaiah 53:7 and 8, but could not understand to whom this passage was referring to. Then let us carefully note what we are told at verse 35, for Philip begins his preaching of the gospel, by preaching Jesus to him. We have seen already that the central focus of the gospel is God's Son, particularly the fact of His death for our sins, His burial, and His resurrection from the dead the third day. Since we then see Philip, as now an apostle, baptize the court official in water immersion, then we know for sure that the Ethiopian man had now come to know God in salvation. And please not here that it is Philip himself who does the baptizing in water. This particular account of Philip then closes with God telling us that Philip preached the gospel in all the cities from Azotus to Caesarea, which was where he is being sent to by God and where he was now to reside.

The last mention of this man Philip in God's word is at Acts 21:8, where we are told, "On the next day we left and came to Caesarea, and entering the house of Philip the evangelist, who was one of the seven, we stayed with him." Earlier in the chapter, when we looked at this verse, we started our examination of Philip by noting that he was part of the original seven deacons chosen by the believers of the local church at Jerusalem, to assist the apostles by looking after the temporal affairs of the church. Now we close our look of Philip by noting that Philip is still at Caesarea, where God had sent him to years before, and most importantly for our purpose now, he is here called an evangelist by God! And if someone was going to ask at this point: How could he go from being an apostle to being an evangelist? The answer to that question, which hopefully by now all readers would be able to answer, is that God has now made a transition, from apostles to evangelists, using Philip as His example to us. What this also means then is that whereas Philip was earlier seen to have God's supernatural sign gifts accompany his ministry of preaching the gospel as an apostle, now all such sign gifts would have ceased in his ministry of preaching the gospel as an evangelist!

What is also important to keep in mind here is that the "we" at Acts 21:8 is a reference to Luke, whom God used to write the book of Acts, plus the apostle Paul, who was here on his journey to Antioch in Syria, as he was completing his third excursion abroad, and also including the men mentioned at Acts 20:4, "where we read, "And he was accompanied by Sopater of Berea, the son of Pyrrhus, and by Aristarchus and Secundus of the Thessalonians, and Gaius of Derbe, and Timothy, and Tychicus and Trophimus of Asia." And for our purpose here, we need to note that Timothy, whom we will look at next, was already a companion to Paul in gospel ministry by this time.

2) Timothy, the evangelist

We first encounter Timothy in God's word at Acts 16:1, noting here what God there tells us, adding verses 2 and 3 for context," [1] Paul came also to Derbe and to Lystra. And a disciple was there, named Timothy, the son of a Jewish woman who was a believer, but his father was a Greek, [2] and he was well spoken of by the brethren who were in Lystra and Iconium. [3] Paul wanted this man to go with him; and he took him and circumcised him because of the Jews who were in those parts, for they all knew that his father was a Greek." So here God tells us that there was a believer named Timothy at Lystra, who Paul wanted to take along with him, being then on his second excursion abroad from Antioch in Syria in the preaching of the gospel, wherever God was leading him to.

And so we see here that Timothy was already a believer when Paul encounters him, and he is well spoken of by the other believers. What is very important to notice here for our present purpose is that his being "well spoken of" here meant that he was already effective in his ministry of sharing the gospel, which is why Iconium is also mentioned here, because Timothy's gospel ministry at this point was even extending to other outlying cities from Lystra. Therefore, this is why the apostle Paul wanted to take him along with him, for he already knew that God had raised him for gospel ministry! And let us also note that when the apostle Paul is first seen taking Timothy along with him at Acts 16, Timothy is still a young man, as can be gathered from the apostle Paul mentioning his being yet a youth at 1 Timothy 4:12, "Let no one look down on your youthfulness..."

And it is because the apostle Paul had taken Timothy along with him in his ministry of preaching the gospel that we see Timothy mentioned in his letters to various local churches, which were visited only after Acts 16, because that is when Timothy first joined Paul as a traveling companion and ministry partner, with these local churches having then become familiar with Timothy. And so we see that Timothy was not mentioned at 1 Corinthians 1:1 as being with the apostle Paul when he first went to Corinth, however, when the apostle Paul wrote his second letter to the local church at Corinth, now he mentions Timothy as being with him, further telling them at 2 Corinthians 1:19, "For the Son of God, Christ Jesus, who was preached among you by us — by me and Silvanus and Timothy..." Similarly when we see the apostle Paul write letters to Philippi, Colossae, and Thessalonica, we also see Timothy being mentioned as being with Paul in gospel ministry when visiting these cities. But what is important to keep in mind for our present purpose is that Timothy was not there as called of God and sent out as an apostle, but rather, Timothy was there preaching the gospel as an evangelist, as we see from 2 Timothy 4:5, "But you, be sober in all things, endure hardship, do the work of an evangelist, fulfill your ministry."

Therefore, when we read here, "do the work of an evangelist, fulfill your ministry," we are to realize that this was a reference to the preaching of the gospel, as is clear from what the apostle Paul already told the Corinthians at 2 Corinthians 1:19 above, and from what he tells the Philippians about Timothy at Philippians 2:19-22, "[19] But I hope in the Lord Jesus to send Timothy to you shortly, so that I also may be encouraged when I learn of your condition. [20] For I have no one else of kindred spirit who will genuinely be concerned for your welfare. [21] For they all seek after their own interests, not those of Christ Jesus. [22] But you know of his proven worth, that he served with me in the furtherance of the gospel like a child serving his father," and also from what he further tells Timothy directly at 2 Timothy 1:8, "Therefore do not be ashamed of the testimony of our Lord or of me His prisoner, but join with me in suffering for the gospel according to the power of God..." In all these passages here, we see that Timothy was involved in preaching the gospel, which was the work of an evangelist, as it was also for Paul, as an apostle.

And before we close our look at Timothy as being an evangelist, we should note and comment on what the apostle Paul says to him in three passages in particular, beginning at 1 Timothy 1:18, "This command I entrust to you, Timothy, my son, in accordance with the prophecies previously made concerning you, that by them you fight the good fight..." What we want to focus on here is the mention of "the prophecies previously made concerning

146

you," which is no doubt a reference to what the apostle Paul further says to Timothy at 1 Timothy 4:14, "Do not neglect the spiritual gift within you, which was bestowed on you through prophetic utterance with the laying on of hands by the presbytery." Therefore, "the prophecies" would be this "prophetic utterance" now mentioned, which would have been through the elders of the local church at Lystra, who would have been prophets with the sign gift of prophecy, as already mentioned. Such prophets were also seen in the local church at Antioch in Syria at Acts 13:1, as the men who were not being called and sent out as apostles, but were to remain at the local church as elders. What this means then relating to this prophetic utterance by the elders as prophets of the local church at Lystra is that they said something in regards to Timothy and his ministry, which has not been recorded in God's word.

And what would be in view here when the apostle Paul says to Timothy, "the laying on of hands by the presbytery," is when the apostle Paul first took Timothy along with him in gospel ministry, which would have been from Lystra. What this means then is that "the presbytery," who would have laid hands on Timothy, is a reference to the elders of the local church at Lystra. And it is important to note also included the apostle Paul, who with Barnabas had been responsible under God for starting the local church there through the preaching of the gospel, which is clear from what the apostle Paul further says to Timothy at 2 Timothy 1:6, "For this reason I remind you to kindle afresh the gift of God which is in you through the laying on of my hands." Therefore, we are to see that this was not a separate laying on of the apostle's hands upon Timothy, but rather what was done due to the apostle Paul being part of the presbytery mentioned above.

Then as to the mention of "spiritual gift within you," mentioned at 1 Timothy 4:14, which Timothy was not to neglect, which was also "the gift of God," which Timothy is told at 2 Timothy 1:6 "to kindle afresh," we are to note that this was not a reference to The precious Holy Spirit, which Timothy had received the very moment he believed what God revealed in the gospel regarding His Son, nor did it refer to any of the sign gifts, which an apostle had, but which Timothy would not have, being an evangelist. And so what is critical to see here is that what is in view here is

147

the call of God which Timothy received from God, which meant that he was now being officially entrusted with the gospel by God, as we have seen at 1 Thessalonians 2:4, which further meant that God was therefore sending him out as an evangelist. In other words, the spiritual gift here, which only God can give, and which was bestowed at the time the apostle Paul laid hands on him, was the Divine enablement to be able to preach the gospel, which for any other evangelist since then, comes at the moment of God's call, which is when God sends one out to preach the gospel as one's ministry.

The apostle Paul gives evidence of this Divine enablement as an apostle, which would also be true of every man called of God as an evangelist, noting what God tells us at Ephesians 6:19, "and pray on my behalf, that utterance may be given to me in the opening of my mouth, to make known with boldness the mystery of the gospel..." And so we see that apostles, as is true of all evangelists, are given Divine enablement by God to be able to preach the gospel without prior preparation, with God leading one to say what He wanted one to say, since God knows the heart of every person one encounters, and only God can lead one to say what would be needful in relation to the gospel, which a person needs to hear in order to come to know God personally in salvation.

It must ever be remembered here that spiritual gifts can only have their source in God! And so we close this chapter with what God said through the apostle Peter at 1 Peter 4:10,11, especially noting this in relation to what has been said above, "[10] As each one has received a special gift, employ it in serving one another as good stewards of the manifold grace of God. [12] Whoever speaks, is to do so as one who is speaking the utterances of God; whoever serves is to do so as one who is serving by the strength which God supplies; so that in all things God may be glorified through Jesus Christ, to whom belongs the glory and dominion forever and ever. Amen." The "whoever speaks" here at verse 11 would be the apostles and prophets in the early church, followed by the evangelists and shepherd/teachers in the remainder of the church age, each having the gift from God mentioned at verse 10, which involves receiving the supernatural ability to speak the utterances of God at the moment God calls one to service. And this is specifically what would have happened to Timothy at the moment of his call as an evangelist, with the elders, including the apostle Paul, then laying hands on him to confirm their agreement with God's working in him for this enablement, since God would have made them aware of it in their own hearts.

WHAT I SAY WILL NEVER SAVE ANYONE,
NO MATTER HOW NICELY DRESSED UP WITH
FANCY WORDS IT MIGHT BE SAID.
ONLY WHAT GOD SAYS THROUGH ME
REGARDING HIS SON, FOCUSED ON THE CORE
OF THE GOSPEL MESSAGE, WILL EVER SAVE
ANYONE!

SECTION FIVE

CLEARING UP SOME MISCONCEPTIONS
RELATING TO EVANGELISM

THE RELATION BETWEEN REPENTANCE AND FAITH

In this chapter, we need to deal with an area which has confused many believers, as to what the relation is between repentance and faith, and as a result this has impacted how one does evangelism. What is key to see here is that while repentance and faith are both necessary in the process of one coming to know God in salvation, nevertheless these are but two sides of the same coin. In other words, what is to be grasped here is that when a sinner repents, one is at the same time coming to believe in God, with the reverse also being true, namely that when one believes in God for salvation, one has repented. Repentance and faith are BOTH works of God, which He does simultaneously, meaning both at the same time, when He brings a person to a personal relationship with Himself in salvation.

Verses which we can look at here, first in regards to repentance, are Acts 11:18, where we read, "When they heard this, they quieted down and glorified God, saying, "Well then, God has granted to the Gentiles also the repentance that leads to life;" " then also 2 Corinthians 7:10, "For the sorrow that is according to the will of God produces a repentance without regret, leading to salvation, but the sorrow of the world produces death;" and then noting what God also tells us at 2 Timothy 2:25, "with gentleness correcting those who are in opposition, if perhaps God may grant them repentance leading to the knowledge of the truth..." The word "repentance" in all three of these verses is the same Greek word, which speaks of a work of God whereby a sinner experiences a change of mind and heart toward God, which means turning 180 degrees from going one's own way in sin to now turning to God to receive from Him the forgiveness of sins and eternal life with Him.

And then verses which we can look at in regards to faith in God are noting what God says to us at Acts 15:8,9, "[8] And God, who knows the heart, testified to them giving them the Holy Spirit, just as He also did to us; [9] and He made no distinction between us and them, cleansing their hearts by faith;" then also Ephesians 2:8-10, "[8] For by grace you have been saved through faith; and that not of yourselves, it is the gift of God; [9] not as a result of works, so that no one may boast. [10] For we are His workmanship, created in Christ Jesus for good works, which God prepared beforehand so that we would walk in them;" then also at Hebrews 12:2, "fixing our eyes on Jesus, the author and perfecter of faith, who for the joy set before Him endured the cross, despising the shame, and has sat down at the right hand of the throne of God;" and then also at 2 Peter 1:1, "Simon Peter, a bond-servant and apostle of Jesus Christ, to those who have received a faith of the same kind as ours, by the righteousness of our God and Savior, Jesus Christ:" In each of these passages, the word "faith" is the same Greek word, which speaks of a work of God in leading a sinner to come to believe in Him for the forgiveness of sins and eternal life with Him.

What we are to therefore grasp in regards to repentance and faith in evangelism is that we are to share the gospel as God leads us, to whom God leads us, and He will take the gospel shared and work repentance and faith in a sinner to bring that sinner to a personal knowledge of Himself in salvation! And here we would be helped in again mentioning what God's precious Son, Jesus Christ, told unbelievers when on earth, namely the truth shared at John 6:44 and 65, where we read, "[44] No one can come to Me unless the Father who sent Me draws him; and I will raise him up on the last day... [65] For this reason I have said to you, that no one can come to Me unless it has been granted him from the Father." Salvation is wholly a work of God, as we have seen; therefore it should not surprise us that repentance and faith, two important elements in that salvation, are also a work of God.

EVANGELISM IS NOT JUST FOR THE EVANGELIST TO DO

Another area of confusion among believers is the thinking that evangelism, in terms of sharing the faith with unbelievers, is mostly the task of the evangelists to do. While it is no doubt true that evangelists are called of God to preach the gospel, as the main reason for being sent out from a local church by God, nevertheless, it is not in keeping with God's will, as expressed in His word, to think that this leaves the rest of believers free from sharing their faith. Since God calls all human beings to procreate within the context of marriage so as to keep the human race going in the physical world, then too is it God's will for all His children to reproduce spiritually through being vessels in His Hands for that to happen.

We have already seen from 2 Corinthians 5:14 to 6:2 in the first chapter of Section Three that God indeed wants all believers involved in sharing the faith with others, starting in one's home and expanding from there, to one's relatives and friends, and co-workers and acquaintances, as God leads and directs. Now we need to reinforce that truth here with other examples from God's word, where we see this to indeed be true. For instance, at Acts 8, immediately after the martyrdom of Stephen at Acts 7, we have a persecution which breaks out against the local church at Jerusalem, with the result that all the believers are scattered from Jerusalem, noting what we read at Acts 8:1-4, and especially noting what these believers did as they were scattered, "[1] Saul was in hearty agreement with putting him to death. And on that day a great persecution began against the church in Jerusalem, and they were all scattered throughout the regions of Judea and Samaria, except the apostles. [2] Some devout men buried Stephen, and made loud lamentation over him. [3] But Saul began ravaging the church, entering house after house, and dragging off men and women, he would put them in prison. [4] Therefore, those who had been scattered went about preaching the word." Please note the important information we are being given here in the second part of verse 1, namely that "all" the believers of the local church at Jerusalem were scattered, "except the apostles." And at verse 4, we are told that these believers shared their faith with others wherever they were scattered. It is clear here that this was not done by the apostles, the very men whom God had appointed for the task, but rather, this was being done by believers who did not have such a call to public ministry upon their lives, but who nevertheless did what it was in God's plan for them to do.

God gives us a further account of these same scattered believers at Acts 11:19-21, noting there what we further learn, "[19] So then those who were scattered because of the persecution that occurred in connection with Stephen made their way to Phoenicia and Cyprus and Antioch, speaking the word to no one except to Jews alone. [20] But there were some of them, men of Cyprus and Cyrene, who came to Antioch and began speaking to the Greeks also, preaching the Lord Jesus. [21] And the hand of the Lord was with them, and a large number who believed turned to the Lord." As we see at verse 21, God was obviously pleased with what these scattered believers were doing since many people came to know God in a personal relationship in salvation through their sharing their faith in God's precious Son, Jesus Christ. Being a vessel in God's Hands to bring a child into this world is no doubt one of the joys one can experience in this life. But let us not stop there. Let us also all experience the joy of seeing a person on one's way to a lost eternity pass from death to life, as a result of one coming to know God in salvation, noting what God tells us at John 5:24, which is one of my favorite verses, "Truly, truly, I say to you, he who hears My word, and believes Him who sent Me, has eternal life, and does not come into judgment, but has passed out of death into life."

THE WORD "MISSIONARY" IS A MISNOMER

There are a number of words which believers commonly use which are not found in God's word. One of them is the word 'pastor,' which is a product of translators. The Biblical word is "shepherd/teachers," which are mentioned at Ephesians 4:11, after the mention of the "evangelists." Even the word 'evangelism,' as part of the title of this book is not a Biblical word, although it has found its way into our vocabulary in regards to sharing the Christian faith with those who are unbelievers. And now in this chapter, we need to mention the word 'missionary,' as being another word which Christians are very familiar with, and even the cults, but which is not a Biblical word. Many Biblical translations use the term to indicate the three excursions abroad of the apostle Paul from the local church at Antioch in Syria, calling these his first, second, and third missionary journeys. What one does not realize here is that in doing so, one is really obscuring the true role of an apostle, and later of an evangelist. In other words, when one calls an apostle or an evangelist a missionary, one can easily lose track of the fact that these men are really apostles and evangelists. Believers then become fairly familiar with what a missionary does, but loses track of what is an evangelist, and what an evangelist does.

Another problem with the use of the word 'missionary,' when the word "evangelist" should be used, is that one then develops a picture of a missionary and thinks that going abroad to preach the gospel is all an evangelist does, when one finds out that a missionary is really an evangelist. As we have seen in the previous section, an evangelist has the preaching of the gospel as a main task from God, to be sure, but that is not all an evangelist does. Since the word 'missionary' is not in the Bible, then one really never does associate these other tasks, such as the important task of teaching, with an evangelist, and so the full role of an evangelist gets lost or obscured.

Yet another problem which needs to be mentioned in the use of the word 'missionary,' instead of evangelist, is that one easily loses track of the fact that evangelists raised of God are always only men. When one looks at the modern missionary movement, one sees many women as being on the mission field. As we have noted earlier in the book, evangelists, as were the apostles before them (1 Corinthians 9:5), were allowed to take a believing wife along with them when they traveled abroad from the local church. However, we never see the wives ever go out on their own. Such a practice is foreign to the mind of God, although in these last days of the church age, we do see women not only calling themselves missionaries, but even evangelists. When we use the term 'missionary' instead of "evangelist," we are making it harder to focus on the Biblical truth associated with the word "evangelist."

A LAST WORD

As we come to the end of the book, we should mention here that it likely has not escaped most readers that a lot of what has been written in this book is not being seen today, simply because we are in the last days of the church age, where ignorance of the truth, perversion of the truth, and even setting aside of the truth, reigns. If one is not convinced of this, then please obtain and read my third book, entitled "How We Know For Sure That We Are Living In The Last Days."

At around 90 AD, which was only about 60 years after the church started on earth, God had the apostle John write to the local church at Ephesus, which was representative of the churches at the beginning of the church age, what we read at Revelation 2:4, "But I have this against you, that you have left your first love." And their first love here was the truth of God's word, which believers on earth had already departed from, a scant 60 years after the church had started! Then at Revelation 3:20, God again has the apostle John write to a local church, this time at Laodicea, which was representative of churches of the last days of the church age, and there says, "Behold, I stand at the door and knock; if anyone hears My voice and opens the door, I will come in to him and will dine with him, and he with Me." Here we note that God is speaking of the state of the church in our own day, because we are no doubt living in the last days, and we see that believers now are not even aware that God's Son is no longer ever present by The Holy Spirit in the gathering of the local church! It is no longer just a departure from God's word, but now it is a departure from The Word made flesh, God's precious Son, Jesus Christ, Himself! Let us remember these things as we await His soon return from Heaven to earth.

To God alone be all praise, honor, and glory, with thanksgiving, both now and forevermore! Amen, amen, and amen.

LEADING A PERSON TO FAITH IN GOD IS NEVER IN ACCORDANCE WITH A FORMULA OF OUR OWN DESIGN; BUT RATHER, ALWAYS A WORKING OF GOD IN GRACE AND POWER THROUGH ONE OF HIS CHILDREN ON EARTH AS AN AVAILABLE VESSEL!

ADDENDUM

SOME GOOD NEWS FOR THOSE WHO MAY NOT AS YET BE PART OF THE FAMILY OF GOD

Possibly one has been reading this book and has become aware of not knowing this God Who created us and gave us physical life into this world, and up to now has allowed you to live on earth. However, you do have the desire to know God in a personal way. If this is the case, then this chapter has been written specifically for you. And what God wants you to have in coming to know Him is the peace and joy which comes in knowing that all of your sins committed in your lifetime are forgiven and that you have eternal life with God. And so, your greatest need at the moment is to make peace with God so as to go to Heaven, which is God's eternal home. And so this chapter will help to bring that about by pointing you to God so as to come to faith in Him.

And as we begin, we need to note a most important promise which God makes at Romans 6:23 to all those who do not yet know Him, "For the wages of sin is death, but the free gift of God is eternal life in Christ Jesus our Lord." The good news here is that God offers you eternal life with Him as a free gift, which is to be obtained in His Son, Jesus Christ. What God does not do in this verse from the Bible is tell us how to obtain that eternal life with Him.

Another verse that we can look at where God does let us know how one can obtain that eternal life with Him is noting what God tells us at John 3:16, "For God so loved the world, that He gave His only begotten Son, that whoever believes in Him shall not perish, but have eternal life." Now the added truth which God makes known here is that the eternal life, which He gives to a human being as a free gift, is for those who believe in His Son.

Then the question is: What is it that I am to believe about God's Son, Jesus Christ, which will lead God to give me eternal life with Him forever? And the beauty of God is that He never leaves us guessing, especially when it comes to having a personal relationship with Him, which He desires us to have. Therefore, we should not be surprised when God gives us the answer to our question in what He tells us at 1 Corinthians 15:1-4, "[1] Now I make known to you, brethren, the gospel which I preached to you, which also you received, in which also you stand, [2] by which also you are saved, if you hold fast the word which I preached to you, unless you believed in vain. [3] For I delivered to you as of first importance what I also received, that Christ died for our sins according to the Scriptures, [4] and that He was buried, and that He was raised on the third day according to the Scriptures..." Therefore, "the gospel," which simply means 'good news,' which God wants you to hear and believe in order to "be saved," which simply refers to you coming to know God and have eternal life with Him, is that His Son has already died for you, has already been buried, and has already been raised from the dead again the third day after His death, in order that God would have a basis by which to forgive you of all your sins, which are all against Him, and to freely give you eternal life with Him, for simply believing this message in your heart.

One thing which often prevents a person from believing the gospel at this point is not seeing oneself as a sinner before a Holy God. When we look at ourselves by our own assessment, and especially when we compare ourselves with others around us, we often think of ourselves as being better than others, and so good enough to enter Heaven in our present condition. The problem with this is that it is the product of our own thinking and is not God's assessment of our situation. God's assessment of our situation is as He tells us at Romans 3:10-12,23 in part, "[10] as it is written, "There is none righteous, not even one...

168

[11] there is none who seeks for God [12] all have turned aside... there is none who does good, there is not even one... [23] for all have sinned and fall short of the glory of God..." Quite a different assessment of the human race from that which we as human beings often have of ourselves, is this not? But why would God have such an assessment of the whole human race? For the answer to that question, we need to be aware that God is Creator of all that exists, so that when God created the first man, Adam, at the beginning of time, God created him in innocence, meaning that Adam as first created by God neither knew good nor evil, nor was there any sin anywhere in God's original sinless creation.

However, the day came when God tested Adam with a command, saying to him in the garden of Eden here on earth, which was the perfect environment which God had for him, what we now read at Genesis 2:16,17, "The Lord God commanded the man, saying, "From any tree of the garden you may eat freely; [17] but from the tree of the knowledge of good and evil you shall not eat, for in the day that you eat from it you will surely die." How important to see here that God gave Adam, who although a real person was also representative of the whole human race, the warning of the penalty of death for disobedience to His command.

Unfortunately, the day did come when Adam did partake of the forbidden tree and thereby did sin against God. The moment that happened, Adam not only became a sinner by practice, but also a sinner by nature. One thing my parents had to continually do while under their care was to restrain me from continually going the wrong way, for it seemed that of myself I could not do good, but kept going into sin. The reason this was happening is that from the age of accountability onwards, I had not only become a sinner by practice, but also a sinner by nature. And here the age of accountability needs to be seen as being when as a young child in innocence - which moment is known only by God - one comes to learn the right from the wrong and chooses the wrong, thereby becoming personally accountable to God for one's own sin against Him, since all sin is first of all against Him. And that is why God can say at Romans 3:23 above that "all have sinned and fall short of the glory of God," because God knows that all human beings will go the way of Adam, our representative man, which is also why God can say what He does in regards to the whole of the human race at Romans 5:12, where we read, "Therefore, just as through one man (Adam) sin entered into the world, and death through sin, and so death spread to all men, because all sinned" (from the age of accountability onward).

And so we see that the whole human race is declared by God to not only be sinners by practice and by nature from the age of accountability onwards, but the whole of the human race is now subject to death! In other words, in God's sight the whole of the human race is under the judgment of the penalty of death, due to all being sinners by practice and by nature. You will recall above, in the first verse we quoted from Romans 6:23, God did say there that "the wages of sin is death." And what God means by "death" here is not just loss of physical life, when the physical body we have dies, but also has spiritual death in mind, which is far worse! Spiritual death has its beginning when a separation takes place between a person and God at the moment one becomes a sinner at the age of accountability and ends after the final judgment of time, when God forever casts away from His Presence those who before physical death refused to believe in His Son, Jesus Christ, thereby personally forfeiting the forgiveness of their sins and eternal life with God. And now all such will pay the penalty for their own sins in hell, away from the Presence of God forever.

It is in the midst of such a hopeless situation in which the whole of the human race found itself in that God TOOK THE INITIATIVE and sent His own eternally existing Son into the world, as born of a virgin in the innocence of Adam — so as not to inherit the sinful nature passed on from generation after generation from Adam onwards — so that He might be the acceptable sacrifice offered to God His Father at the cross, there bearing our sins in His body, and there dying the death due our sins! God's Son, Jesus Christ, was then buried and raised from the dead the third day, to ever be alive, for it is through Him, on the basis of what God has done for us through His Son, that God The Father forgives our sins and imparts us eternal life.

170

Now, by God's grace and His enablement, may you see your need of God's Son to be Your Savior from the penalty due sin, which is death, not only physical, but also spiritual. And by God's grace, may He lead you to believe in His Son, Jesus Christ, and in believing, to receive the forgiveness of your sins and eternal life with Him forever! And based on the truth just shared, the author would now like to ask you a few questions, with the answer being just between yourself and God:

When God says at Romans 3:23, "for all have sinned and fall short of the glory of God," does that include you?

When God says at Romans 5:8, "But God demonstrates His own love toward us, in that while we were yet sinners, Christ died for us," were you included in Christ's death on behalf of sinners?

And when God further says at 1 Peter 3:18 in part, "For Christ also died for sins once for all, the just for the unjust, so that He might bring us to God, having been put to death in the flesh, but made alive in the spirit," were you part of the unjust for whom Christ died?

When God says at Romans 6:23, "For the wages of sin is death, but the free gift of God is eternal life in Christ Jesus our Lord," do you want that eternal life as a free gift from God?

When God says at John 3:16, "For God so loved the world, that He gave His only begotten Son, that whoever believes in Him shall not perish, but have eternal life," do you now believe that Jesus Christ is indeed God's Son in human flesh, Who came from Heaven to this earth to die in your place, so as to save you from ever experiencing the judgment of God leading to an eternal separation from God in hell?

And when God then further says to you at Isaiah 55:6, "Seek the Lord while He may be found; call upon Him while He is near," for His further promise to you here is as we read at Romans 10:9-11,13, "[9] that if you confess with your mouth Jesus as Lord, and believe in your heart that God raised Him from the dead, you will be saved (that is, you will now enter into a personal relationship with God by faith); [10] for with the heart a person believes, resulting in righteousness (that is, in now receiving God's own righteous life to live by), and with the mouth he confesses, resulting in salvation (that is, in now receiving as a free gift the forgiveness of sins and eternal life with God). [11] For the Scripture says, "Whoever believes in Him will not be disappointed…" [13] for "Whoever will call on the name of the Lord will be saved." Will you now call upon God from your heart, telling God in your own words your answer to each question that has just been asked?

The author's prayer for you at this point, as you now call upon God by His grace, is what we read at Romans 15:13, "Now may the God of hope fill you with all joy and peace in believing, so that you will abound in hope by the power of the Holy Spirit."

THE NEXT BOOK

God has given His approval to two new books, the one being titled, "Father, Forgive Them, For They Know What They Are Doing." The author's third book deals with the fact that the end of the present age is very close. This book picks up from there and will examine WHY God's judgment will fall on this present world. In other words, when God's judgment comes, and we can be absolutely sure that it is coming, then no one of all mankind facing that judgment will be able to say that it was not justified. All throughout history, God has destroyed one nation after another due to the sins of those nations. This was meant as a history lesson for those nations which come afterwards. In this book, we will also examine this history lesson from God and apply it to our own day. This is a book you will not want to miss, if you are concerned about the current events in the world and are wondering what this world is coming to! This will be the author's eighth book in the Truth Seeker's Library™ series.

The second book God has given His approval to is titled, "The Beginning Of A New Dawn." This will be the author's first book in a new series called, "The Christian Fiction Library™ series. This book is a love story within a love story, which should be of interest to every woman, as the main character is a woman, but which should also be of interest to men, since the lover is a man, and also because there are a number of interesting technical details provided, due to the author having an Engineering background.

As this book is being published, I am still not sure which of the above two books will be written first. What one can do is look at my website http://www.pilgrimpathwaypublications.com, where I try to keep readers current on what is being written.

NOTES

Proof

Made in the USA
Charleston, SC
26 January 2015